Christmas Delights
Quilts That Celebrate the Season

JAYNETTE HUFF

Martingale®
& COMPANY

Christmas Delights: Quilts That Celebrate the Season
© 2003 Jaynette Huff

That Patchwork Place®
is an imprint of Martingale & Company®.

Martingale & Company
20205 144th Avenue NE
Woodinville, WA 98072-8478
www.martingale-pub.com

CREDITS

President . . . . Nancy J. Martin
CEO. . . . . Daniel J. Martin
Publisher . . . . Jane Hamada
Editorial Director . . . . Mary V. Green
Managing Editor . . . . Tina Cook
Technical Editor . . . . Ellen Pahl
Copy Editor. . . . . Karen Koll
Design Director . . . . Stan Green
Illustrator. . . . . Laurel Strand
Cover and Text Designer . . . . Stan Green
Photographer. . . . . Brent Kane

Printed in China
08 07 06 05 04   8 7 6 5 4 3 2

DEDICATION

This book is dedicated to my sisters-in-law, Shirley Johnson and Lorraine Gabbert. They welcomed me into the family and into their hearts the first day I met them. And also to my husband, Larry, my encourager and supporter. I love you all.

ACKNOWLEDGMENTS

Julia Dascanio once again stepped in to serve as block tester and quiltmaker. She makes my job so much easier. I enjoy her involvement and assistance and value the precision and high quality of her workmanship.

Thank you to Valerie Schraml for her continued computer assistance. I truly count on her ability to transform my words into the correct manuscript format.

To the people at Martingale & Company, especially Mary Green, who continue to allow me to develop my ideas and designs and to share them with others in a book. It is such a wonderful feeling when they become enthusiastic about the same things that excite me. I am very grateful for their professional encouragement and acceptance.

And thanks to all of you who like my designs and who continue to support my efforts! May all your Christmas holidays be joyous!

Library of Congress Cataloging-in-Publication Data

Huff, Jaynette.
   Christmas delights : quilts that celebrate the season / Jaynette Huff.
      p. cm.
   ISBN 1-56477-488-0
   1. Patchwork—Patterns. 2. Quilting. 3. Holiday decorations. I. Title.
   TT835 .H7896 2003
   746.46'041—dc21
                                                2002156271

Contents

Celebrate the Yuletide Season of Your Senses

YULETIDE IS THE SEASON OF OUR SENSES. Christmas—we can see its beauty. We hear its joy. We can reach out and feel its warmth. We taste its goodness. We inhale its aromas. Christmas is the season for sensory delight. It is a time for the reawakening of all our senses. There is so much to savor, to take in, to anticipate, and to remember.

This Yuletide season, fully experience all your senses. Breathe deeply. Feast the eyes. Inhale the aromas. Savor the tastes. Listen for the sounds. Remember the good times. Push the buttons of sensory delight to the fullest. Then channel that delight into the quilts you create.

Our quilts are much more than simply the fabric, batting, and threads we use. They are even more than simply our time. Our quilts are actually a wonderful celebration of our best thoughts and anticipations of how our works will be received and used. They are also an appreciation for those loved ones who are now gone but who are remembered and cherished.

Ultimately our quilts are a reflection of ourselves—our talents, our imaginations, our joys, our memories, and our love. Let this Christmas season be a quilted one of sensory celebration.

Celebrate the season with quilts!

Catch the Christmas Quilting Spirit

TOOLS AND SUPPLIES

There is an overwhelming abundance of sewing supplies and equipment available for today's quilter. Below you will find a listing and brief discussion of those that are useful to paper foundation piecing as presented in this book.

Colored markers. Thin-line, colored markers for making reference marks on your foundation paper. Four or five different colors are recommended.

Embellishments. Buttons, beads, charms, miniature ornaments, embroidery floss, ribbons, laces. Use them to your heart's content.

Freezer paper. The recommended paper for the foundation. Commercially available.

Iron and ironing board. Set up within easy reach as you will use it following every fabric addition. Steam setting is preferred.

Light box. For easier tracing of the pattern onto freezer paper foundation. You may also use a window, or create your own. Later used to trace embellishment placement lines.

Mechanical pencil. For tracing the pattern onto freezer paper foundation.

Scissors. One good-quality pair that you are willing to use for cutting both paper and fabric. Smaller embroidery size works especially well for easy pickup and trimming.

Sewing pins. Extra long, fine, silk glass-head pins are recommended. Used to secure the parts together when matching, and later for sashing and border attachment. Do not sew over, but do not remove until the last moment to prevent slippage of the layers.

Stiletto. Sharply pointed instrument that helps separate stubbornly adhered paper and fabric pieces.

Tweezers. For easier paper foundation removal in those tiny, hard-to-reach corners and crevices.

In addition to the specific items needed for paper piecing, you'll need the basic sewing and quilting supplies listed below.

Batting. Choose from cotton or a blend of cotton and polyester. Cotton batting is best for machine quilting.

Beading needle. For bead embellishment.

Darning foot, or open-toe appliqué foot. For free-motion machine quilting.

Even-feed foot, or walking foot. For straight-line machine quilting.

Fabric markers. For marking quilting designs.

Machine needle, size 80/12 or 90/14. For piecing.

Hand or machine quilting needles of your choice.

Rotary-cutting equipment: cutter, mat, and rulers. Choose a mat at least 17" x 23" for easy strip cutting of borders. A 6" x 24" ruler with ⅛" marks is recommended for cutting strips. A 6" x 6" square ruler is handy for trimming pattern parts and sections, and a 12½" x 12½" square is helpful to square up your work.

Safety pins, size 0 or size 1. Use these sizes only, for pin basting.

Seam ripper. For removing stitches when incorrectly sewn.

Sewing machine in good running order. The stitching required is a simple straight stitch forward and back. Recommended stitch length is 15 to 20 stitches per inch.

Thread. Several types are needed.

★ Embroidery floss. Commercially available. Used for block embellishment and detail outline.

★ Machine quilting thread. Nylon monofilament thread. Clear for light fabrics, and smoke for dark fabrics.

★ Machine piecing thread. A good-quality 100%-cotton thread in a neutral color. Used for piecing all blocks and borders. Usually a neutral tan or gray works well, as the colors blend with most of the fabrics used.

FABRIC SELECTION AND PREPARATION

One of the greatest joys in making a Christmas quilt is selecting the fabric. There are so many wonderful holiday fabrics: the traditional reds and greens; luscious Christmas florals of poinsettias, roses, and pine boughs; whimsical holiday motifs of Santas and elves, children and toys; and much more.

Now is the time to indulge those senses of sight and touch. Let your imagination soar as you begin to turn your quilts from dreams into reality. Be bold! Be festive! Be whimsical! Be fun! Be joyous! Be whatever your senses tell you to be!

With paper foundation piecing, keep in mind the following guidelines and suggestions for fabric selection. Always prewash your fabrics. It is much easier to prewash fabrics than to endure the heartache of unexpected and disastrous shrinkages and dye runs after you've spent all the time cutting and piecing your project.

★ Use only top-quality 100%-cotton fabrics. Don't waste your time and energy with poor quality fabrics.

★ Provide contrast in value, scale, and intensity (see "Basic Color Principles" on page 7). All three add interest, variety, and life to your work.

★ Look for a variety of tone-on-tone prints, tiny allover prints, coordinated companion fabrics, and solids. They provide visual interest, texture, and design, but they do not detract from the shape of the characters or objects themselves.

★ Use caution with directional prints, large-scale prints and bold geometrics, or big plaids and busy stripes. There is nothing inherently wrong with these prints, but if you use them, work with them carefully. Consider saving them for corner squares, sashing, and borders.

★ Let the Christmas theme be a major factor when making your fabric choices. Use holiday fabrics to set the holiday mood and create a theme for each quilt.

★ Use a border print to set your theme and color palette. Let the last fabric to be used in the quilt be the first one chosen. Christmas and holiday border prints do the work of color selection for you. The fabric designer has already created both the color palette and the various proportions of colors in that palette. When border prints are used as the sashing or outer border, they pull a quilt together.

★ Use colors and fabrics that please you. Trust yourself, and enjoy your unique combination.

★ Consider using special fabrics, such as satins and Ultrasuedes, for special effect or texture, such as in the lettering. Read the manufacturer's instructions for care and use, and test for colorfastness.

Today we are so fortunate to have such a luscious abundance of beautiful cotton fabrics. Step out and immerse yourself in them! Respond to your senses of sight and touch. Indulge yourself, and create a Christmas delight!

Try It!

Use what works for you. If it has been successful in the past, continue. However, if it is a new or different approach or suggestion, give it a try. Keep in mind, this is a journey, and we all learn along the way. And remember, if you don't have a particular tool you desire, maybe Santa will bring it to you this Christmas. Put it on your wish list!

TERMINOLOGY

This section contains an alphabetic listing and brief definition of the various terms and phrases encountered throughout this book. Some contain specific page references to more complete explanations.

Dashed lines. Marks used to separate the pattern parts when a pattern must be stitched in segments. These are cutting lines. See page 9.

Fabric key. The table provided with each block description that lists all fabrics needed. Each fabric is identified with a capital letter or letters; for example, *S* means star print.

Foundation pattern. The complete pattern on which you actually sew. It contains the sewing lines and parts as well as the fabric designations and sewing order. It can be made of various materials, but freezer paper is recommended for the patterns in this book.

Hash marks or reference marks. Pre-sewing marks that are added to your foundation sheet on every dashed line. The rule is: "Dashes need hashes." These reference marks will be used later to "pinpoint match" the sewn parts so that they go together exactly.

Paper foundation piecing. An organized step-by-step process of piecing fabrics together in alphabetic and numeric order directly onto a paper foundation on which the sewing lines have been drawn. See "Successful Paper Foundation Piecing" on page 7.

Part. An organized collection of pattern pieces that should be sewn as a unit. Parts are separated from each other on the pattern by short dashed lines.

Piece. The smallest unit within a pattern, made up of just one fabric piece.

Pin-checking. A quick test to see if enough fabric has been allowed for flipping over later with complete coverage of a particular pattern piece. Pin along the proposed sewing line, and then check by flipping up the new fabric piece to see if it will be big enough.

Pinpoint matching. A technique for ensuring that the pattern parts are correctly aligned. Using the hash marks, insert a sewing pin straight through the top of a hash mark and fabric of one part and into the corresponding fabric and hash mark of the second part. If correctly aligned, they will match.

Reverse or mirror image. The pattern that is the mirror image of an original drawing. Create by drawing the reverse image of the foundation.

Sewing order. The step-by-step listing of the order in which you sew or piece the pattern. It is the alphabetic and numeric recipe to the piecing of each pattern (e.g. Part A: 1–3). On the foundation patterns, it is indicated by a boldface capital letter and number.

Solid lines. Used to indicate separate pattern pieces within each part. Solid lines are sewing lines. Do not cut along these lines.

Squaring up. The process of ensuring straight sides and 90° angles in corners.

Stay stitching. A line of stitching ⅛" from the edge of a block that stabilizes the outer edges. It prevents the bias edges of your block from stretching until you add borders or binding.

Swatch chart. A visual guide to your fabric key. Attach actual pieces of your fabrics to a chart and label each with the corresponding alphabetic symbol and verbal description (page 8).

Basic Color Principles

Value. Value is the difference between the lightness and darkness of colors. Within your quilt, incorporate fabrics of light, medium, and dark values. Of course, value is a relative term. The fabric of darkest value in one quilt may be of only medium value in another.

Scale. Scale refers to the size of the designs printed on the fabrics. Variety in scale adds interest to a quilt. When choosing your fabrics, select large-, medium-, and small-scale prints. Scale, like value, is relative. What is considered small in one quilt may be medium in another. In addition, what is appropriate scale will vary with factors such as block design and piecing technique. Due to the smaller block size of some of these patterns, large-scale prints are probably inappropriate for the blocks, but not for the sashing, corner squares, or borders.

Intensity. How brilliant or intense are the colors of your chosen fabrics? A little bit of bright or strong intensity can go a long way, but its absence can shroud your quilt in dullness and boredom. A touch of color intensity can make your quilt eye-catching and memorable.

Successful Paper Foundation Piecing

Each block in this book follows the same paper-piecing construction process. Simply follow the alphabetic and numeric sewing order. Read on for specific directions to create your own Christmas magic with perfection guaranteed!

Step 1: Make a Swatch Chart

The first step in the paper foundation piecing process is to make a fabric swatch chart. This organizational step provides order and guidance as the patterns become more elaborate and more fabric variety is introduced. You may be tempted to skip this step, but you will find it to be a lifesaver when you're in the thick of piecing a complex block and are ready to grab the next piece of fabric. A quick check of your swatch chart will let you know if you're on the right track.

Pictured on page 8 is a swatch chart with space for adding identifying labels and letters underneath each box.

Step 2: Trace the Pattern onto the Foundation

Trace the desired pattern or design onto your paper foundation. There are several options for your paper foundation, including standard typing paper, bleached newsprint, tear-away stabilizers, or freezer paper. I recommend ordinary freezer paper due to its adhering qualities. After you iron the fabrics to it, they remain secure and tidily tucked out of the way. It also comes on a roll and you can tear off any length needed. Most of the patterns will fit on one width of freezer paper.

This book includes a foundation pattern for each block design. Each part of the block is labeled with sewing order and fabric designations. This is the pattern on which you actually sew. There are photographs of the blocks on pages 22–36. Notice that the pattern is the mirror image of the photograph or finished block. Everything appears in reverse order. This is as it should be, since you sew on the marked paper side and the

Example:

BK   Background

Make photocopies of this swatch chart and use it for each of your projects.

fabric is on the shiny side. When you turn your work over, you will see that everything is correct.

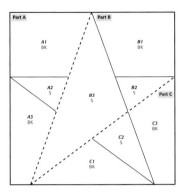

Foundation Pattern

After tracing all the lines (both solid and dashed), be sure to label and number each piece carefully and accurately. Please note that the alphabetic and numeric designations indicate the sewing order (A1, D5, E4) in boldface type; the lighter letters indicate which fabric is to be used (for example, *S* means to use the fabric designated for the star). When you have finished tracing, cut out the entire pattern or block along the outside lines.

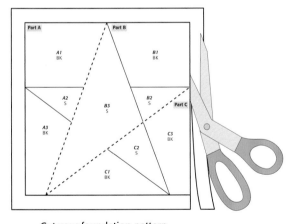

Cut your foundation pattern *on the outer edges.*

Some of the quilts in this book use reversed, or mirror, images of the block designs. To make a mirror image of a block, place the traced or photocopied pattern right side down on a light table or other light source. Place the freezer paper, shiny side down, directly over the foundation pattern. Trace all the lines, dashes, part labels, sewing-order numbers, and fabric designations exactly as given, reversing the numbers and letters so that they are readable.

Step 3: Add Hash Marks to the Foundation

Adding hash marks, or reference marks, to your foundation is an extremely important step. Don't skip this step, because you'll regret it later! On each pattern, individual pieces and parts are separated by solid lines or dashed lines. Solid lines separate pattern pieces within parts. You do not cut along these lines, with the exception of the outer edge of the pattern itself. These are your sewing lines. Short dashed lines separate parts of the pattern within particular blocks. Later you will be cutting the parts apart along the dashed lines.

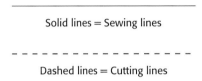

Solid lines = Sewing lines

Dashed lines = Cutting lines

Every dashed line should have reference marks added across it. These marks will later serve as the precise matching points when joining parts. Remember the rule: Dashes need hashes. If it is a dashed line, add reference marks. Use several different types of reference marks—single slash, double slash, triple slash, single X, double X, and so on—to make it very easy to tell which part matches up with the other. Using different color markers will make matching even easier.

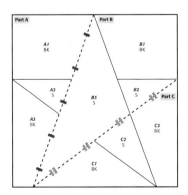

Step 4: Refer to the Sewing Order

Every pattern comes with a sewing order. This is a step-by-step listing of the exact order in which to piece or sew the pattern. It tells you what should be sewn first, what to do with it when it is finished, and when to join various parts.

As you follow the sewing order, place a check mark beside each step as it is completed. This becomes a handy tool for knowing where you were when you stopped last.

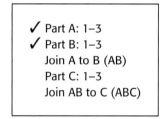

✓ Part A: 1–3
✓ Part B: 1–3
Part C: 1–3
Join A to B (AB)
Part C: 1–3
Join AB to C (ABC)

Sample Sewing Order for Star Block
with Check Marks

Step 5: Cut Out the First Part

After consulting the sewing order, locate the first part listed. Remember, in paper foundation piecing you'll be working both alphabetically and numerically. The more complicated the pattern, the more parts there will be. The sewing order will tell you what is first. Whatever it is, find the first part on your foundation, and with your scissors, carefully cut it out. Attempt to cut exactly on the line. Remember, cut only on dashed lines, not on solid lines. Set the rest of the foundation aside.

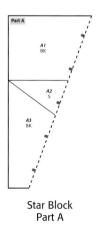

Star Block
Part A

Step 6: Iron the First Piece

Locate the first piece, A1, and its corresponding fabric. Check your swatch chart. From your fabric, roughly cut out a piece large enough to cover that area completely with at least a ¼" seam allowance all around. When in doubt, or especially if you are a beginner, err on the side of too large. With the wrong side of the fabric to the shiny side of the freezer paper, iron the first piece in place over the area marked A1.

Note: This is the only piece that is ironed in place first.

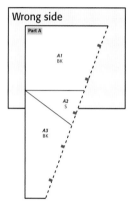

Step 7: Begin Sewing

Look at your foundation to determine which fabric is designated for the second piece, A2. After consulting your swatch chart, cut a piece of the fabric large enough to cover that area. Do not try to cut fabrics the exact size of the piece, as with a template. Instead, cut large enough pieces to ensure coverage with extra for seam allowances. You will be trimming away the excess and can often use the leftovers in another place.

Hold the foundation so the paper side is facing you and the attached fabric piece 1 is behind it. Rotate the paper so that pattern piece A1 is below pattern piece A2. Locate your sewing line. It is the solid straight line running between A1 and A2. With right sides together, place fabric piece 2 over piece 1 with at least ¼" extending beyond the sewing line. With the foundation paper side facing you, hold the whole unit up to the light and "peek." The light showing through will allow you to see if you must reposition your fabric. At this point, most of piece 2 will be hanging down behind piece 1.

Note: The previously sewn work will always be below the line on which you are sewing.

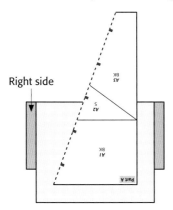

Right side

Again, make sure that the fabric piece you are adding will be large enough to cover the area it is designed to cover, plus extra for seam allowance! Too big is better than too small. It is better to waste a bit of fabric than to have to remove stitches and start again. If you are unsure whether your new piece is large enough, test it first. Simply pin the new fabric along the proposed sewing line and flip the fabric up. You can now see whether it is large enough. This takes only a few seconds but is well worth the effort!

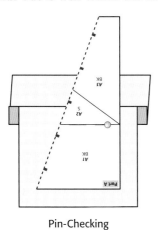

Pin-Checking

With the foundation paper side up, sew along the solid line of the seam, using 15 to 20 stitches per inch. The small stitches will make the removal of the paper foundation easier. When the sewing line begins or ends at the outer edge of the pattern part, begin stitching in the seam allowance area, and continue stitching beyond the pattern edge into the fabric. When the

stitching line intersects another sewing line within the pattern part, stop at the line; backstitch if desired.

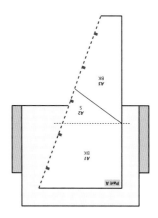

Step 8: Trim the Seam Allowance

Remove the unit from the sewing machine and lay it flat on the table with the foundation side up. With your fingers holding down the previously sewn fabrics, which are still right sides together, carefully fold back the foundation at the sewing line. With your thumbnail, crease the foundation paper along the sewing line. Do not flip up the new fabric yet. Pick up the unit and trim the fabric layers to a scant ¼" seam allowance. Use a small pair of scissors and simply eyeball the ¼". You can also lay the unit on a cutting mat and use a rotary cutter and ruler, if desired.

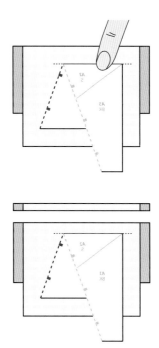

Step 9: Flip and Press

Once you have trimmed the fabrics, fold the foundation paper back down. Flip up the newly attached fabric piece and iron it into place, ensuring a sharp, creased fold along the seam line. Press from the paper side first, gently pulling on the new fabric piece as you glide the iron toward your hand and over the paper. Then turn the whole unit over, check that there are no excess fabric folds or pleats on the seam line, and re-iron from the fabric side.

Check to make sure the entire pattern piece is covered with plenty of extra fabric around the sewing lines. This excess is your seam allowance. If you have a lot of excess fabric, carefully trim it away, making sure you leave plenty around the edges of the piece. This is where you'll really appreciate the freezer paper; it holds the fabrics exactly where you have pressed them and keeps them stable and out of your way.

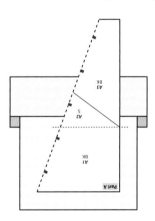

Scrap Saver's Alert

Keep the trimmed pieces for possible use later for smaller pattern pieces.

Step 10: Repeat the Process

Continue in this manner until the entire part is completed. With each new fabric piece, refer to step 7 as needed. Remember to sew the pieces in numeric order or they won't fit together correctly. Continue with step 11 once the entire part has been sewn.

Step 11: Trim the Finished Part

Once an entire part has been sewn, trim an exact ¼" seam allowance around all sides. Accuracy is important here, so use your rotary cutter, mat, and ruler. Do not eyeball this seam allowance.

Next, check the sewing order. You might be instructed to go on to the next part or to sew parts together. It all depends on where you are in the pattern.

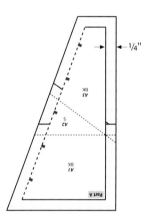

Step 12: Sew the Parts Together

Once several parts are complete, it is time to sew them together. You will need to be as accurate and precise as possible. This is where those hash marks or reference marks that you drew in step 3 really pay off. First, carefully align the appropriate parts with the corresponding hash marks (i.e., single red slashes with single red slashes, double blues with double blues, etc.). Hold them with right sides together.

Next, pinpoint match the reference marks. Using your sewing pins, insert a pin through the hash mark on one part, exactly on the edge of the foundation paper, and then through the fabrics and into the paper of the other part. Ideally, the pin will line up exactly and pierce the corresponding mark on the other part. If it does not, simply reposition the pin and fabrics until it does. Remember, these are bias edges, so they will ease right in. Add as many pins along an edge as you need for exact placement.

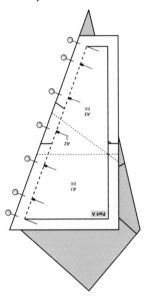

Sew along the pinned edge of the paper. Start at an outside edge and sew to the end of the other outside edge. The needle should just barely brush the paper's edge. Sew carefully, slowly, and accurately. Do not remove the pins until the last moment, or you will lose your perfect match as the pieces shift or slide away from each other.

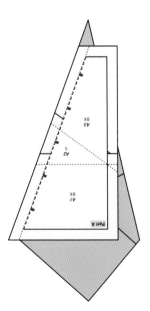

Remove the unit from the sewing machine and check to make sure the points match precisely.

Step 13: Press the Seam Allowances

Once the parts are sewn together, press the seam allowances. The general rule is to let them go where they want to go. Press toward the direction of least resistance. If needed, press the seam allowances open to spread out the bulk of several parts meeting at the same point.

Continue in this manner until all parts are completely joined together, checking the sewing order for guidance.

Step 14: Remove the Paper

Do not remove the foundation paper from the outside edges of any part until it has been joined to other parts, or until the outer edges have been joined to sashing or borders. Remember, these fabrics have been cut and placed with no real concern for grain line, so the edges are primarily bias and can easily stretch or become distorted. To control this, stay stitch ⅛" from the finished block or pattern edges.

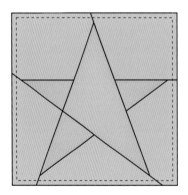

Once other sections stabilize the part, gently remove the foundation paper. Usually the smaller stitch length allows for easy removal, but with tightly adhered pieces, use a stiletto. Gently insert the stiletto point between the paper and fabric and carefully ease it between them, going back and forth to loosen the paper. It may also help to gently bend or roll the paper and fabric unit, loosening the bond between them. Avoid tugging or tearing too hard on the seam lines and stitches.

Be sure to remove all pieces of the foundation, using tweezers to remove paper from tiny corners and crevices.

Step 15: Add Sashing and Borders

The first border or sashing is the most important one because it stabilizes your paper-pieced project and corrals all those tiny bits and pieces.

The beauty of paper foundation piecing should be readily apparent in this step because your blocks and designs are accurate. If sewn correctly, your points will be almost perfect, and there will be ¼" seam allowances all around. The side measurements should all match, so adding sashing and simple borders is a breeze!

Finishing

THE QUILT TOPS ARE COMPLETE, BUT THE FUN IS not over yet! Now you can turn your attention to those final touches that add the sparkle of Christmas, the jingle of bells and beads, the texture of quilting, and the "Christmas card" labeling that tells the quilt's story.

EMBELLISHING, THE FINAL TOUCHES

Embellishment for these holiday projects can truly become the "icing" on the quilt. Here is your chance to loosen up, let it all go, and add the holiday glitz! Many of these designs call for only minimal outline embroidery or buttons, while others call for unlimited embellishment and adornment. Celebrate the season and have fun with these creative touches!

Add embroidery and appliqué details after assembling the quilt top; add buttons, beads, ribbons, and lace after quilting.

Embroidery

Adding some simple hand-embroidery stitches, such as the basic stem stitch, can enhance the features of the designs. The faces of Santa, Mrs. Claus, the snowman, the toy soldier, and the nutcracker all call for embroidery to highlight features such as eyes, mouth, and eyebrows. Embroidery can also provide more color contrast between the fabrics. A simple outline of an edge or part can effectively enhance the shapes, as in the hands of Santa, Mrs. Claus, and the radiant angel.

Simply use the dotted lines on the foundation patterns as a guide for embroidery placement. For some of the blocks, facial designs are provided on the pattern.

You can also use decorative machine-embroidery stitches to enhance your fabrics and blocks. Machine embroider stars and snowflakes in the sky above the snowman or the winter cottage to add festive details that emphasize the spirit of the season.

Stem Stitch

1. Draw the design line lightly on the pieced block using a pencil or water-soluble marker.
2. Cut an 18" length of embroidery floss. Use two strands. Thread your needle and knot the end.
3. Insert the needle into the fabric from the back to the front at point A. As you begin, bury the knot, if possible, behind some darker fabric or gently weave the end into the stitches as you work.
4. Insert the needle at point B and bring it up at point C, halfway between point A and B.

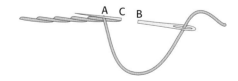

5. Repeat to the end of the drawn line, spacing the stitches evenly. Keep the thread below or to the left of the needle for smooth stitches.
6. Bury the thread end between the fabric layers or weave it into the line of stitching on the wrong side.

Stitcher's Alert

Remember, the fabric pieces and blocks are delicate. Try not to stretch your block or pull the embroidery floss too tight as you stitch.

Couching

Couching is the process of attaching strands of embroidery floss, decorative threads, or cording to fabric by repeatedly stitching over the thread at regular intervals. The nutcracker's jacket and the mane of the rocking horse feature couching.

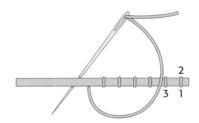

Appliqué

Appliqué is the process of attaching one layer of fabric onto the surface of another layer of fabric. It can be accomplished by hand or machine. You can use it to add decorative detail and dimensionality to the blocks. For instance, Santa, the nutcracker, and the toy soldier all have mustaches appliquéd to their faces. In the quilt "Good Night…Sweet Dreams" on page 57, the candle and flame are appliquéd to Mrs. Claus's candle holder, and appliquéd stick arms hold up the snowman's mittens in "Lawrence Russell, Yuletide Snowman" on page 27. Lines of long and short dashes on the foundation pattern are provided as a guide for making the appliqué templates and for placement. Be sure to add seam allowances if you will be hand appliquéing. Stitch the motif in place using your favorite hand or machine appliqué technique.

Embroidery Placement

Appliqué Placement

Button Placement

Adding a Mane to the Rocking Horse

1. Cut two 24" to 26" lengths of six-strand embroidery floss. Fold the threads in half lengthwise together.

2. Starting with the folded end at the base of the horse's neck, begin looping the threads back and forth up the neck.
3. At each neck loop, couch, or secure, the thread strands with an overstitch, thus attaching the loops at the edge of the neckline, yet allowing the larger, more open loops to remain loose.
4. Leave a ½" to ¾" length of embroidery floss loose at the forehead for the horse's forelock.

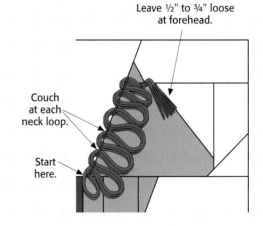

Leave ½" to ¾" loose at forehead.

Couch at each neck loop.

Start here.

Several of the quilts feature panels to express Yuletide wishes and personal holiday greetings. Carefully consider the fabric that you will use. The letters should stand out, be easily read, and remain sharp and clear. Some fabrics are better suited for lettering than others. For the quilts in this book, I used Ultrasuede and fusible appliqué. Ultrasuede adds depth and texture. The edges of the pieces do not ravel; letters and points remain sharp and clear.

You can use hand or machine appliqué, but I designed these panels with the fusible technique in mind. Fuse the letters to the quilt top first; follow the fusing with a more permanent attachment (i.e., machine buttonhole or satin stitch). There are many commercially available fusible webs, and the process is quite easy.

1. Select the message and letters you desire. Be sure to check your spelling carefully. (Refer to pages 92–93 for the letter style shown in this book.)
2. Enlarge or reduce the letters to the appropriate size depending on space allowed and message length.
3. Trace the letters in reverse on the paper side of the fusible webbing.
4. Cut out, allowing an extra ⅛" around each letter.
5. Fuse the letters to the wrong side of the letter fabric, having the adhesive side down and the paper side up.
6. Cut out on the lines, and remove the paper backing from the fusible web.
7. Arrange the letters in the correct placement on the quilt top.
8. Fuse to the quilt top. (Refer to manufacturer's instructions for suggested temperature setting and duration.)
9. For added permanence and beauty, stitch the letters to the quilt top using a satin stitch, straight stitch, or blanket stitch.

Buttons

Buttons are used for the characters' eyes and as block decoration. Consider button additions carefully and choose them specifically to enhance each block and quilt. Refer to the suggested sizes and numbers provided for blocks with button embellishments. Use the shaded button markings on the foundation pattern as a guide for button placement.

Beads

Seed beads, bugle beads, wooden beads, crystal beads, you name it! Beads add sparkle and glitz to your holiday quilts. They can be the buttons on your angel's dress or the decoration on each gingerbread boy and girl. They can enhance the texture of your winter cottage or gingerbread house, or turn a simple pine tree into an ultra-glitzy Christmas tree. The problem will not be in finding locations for the beads, but rather knowing when "enough is enough."

Charms, Ribbons, Miniature Ornaments, and More

Let the fun begin! These Christmas quilts, as well as the season, encourage plentiful use of charms, miniature ornaments, and jewels. The gingerbread house and the Feather Tree Advent Calendar are especially suited for heavy embellishment. If it can be safely and securely attached, and if you like it, add it!

LAYERING AND BASTING

The three layers of your quilt—the top, batting, and backing—need to be temporarily held together by basting. Well-done basting leads to easier quilting later.

1. Prewash the backing fabric and batting if needed. Check the batting manufacturer's instructions.
2. Cut the backing fabric and batting 4" to 6" larger than the pieced top. Several of the quilts require that you sew two or three lengths of fabric together to make a large enough backing. Be sure to trim away the selvage edges before sewing the lengths together. Once sewn, press the seams open.

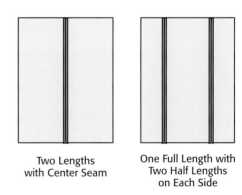

Two Lengths
with Center Seam

One Full Length with
Two Half Lengths
on Each Side

Two Lengths
Pieced Horizontally

3. Place the backing fabric right side down on a flat work surface. Secure with masking tape in several places along the edges.

4. Place the batting on top of the secured backing. Smooth out the batting so that it is flat and free of wrinkles.

5. Center the pieced top, right side up, on the batting and backing. Carefully smooth it out from the center.

6. Baste the layers together, using thread for hand quilting or size 0 or 1 rustproof safety pins for machine quilting. Space basting stitches or pins about 3" to 4" apart.

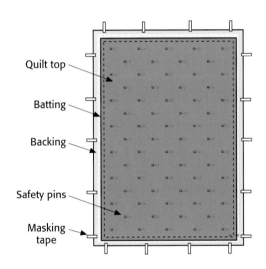

QUILTING

It is not a quilt until it is quilted, and quilting is what appeals to our sense of touch—the "feel" of the quilting. Paper foundation piecing is especially suited to machine quilting; the number and thickness of the seam allowances can make hand quilting more difficult, although not impossible. Following are some suggestions for machine quilting these Christmas designs.

Outline the characters, Yuletide toys, and trinkets. Quilt in the ditch around the outline of each character or object and around each part of a character (i.e., the dress, the apron, the sleeve, etc.).

Quilt each block component as if it were only one piece of fabric. For example, the star in the Yuletide Star block (page 34) is composed of four

pieces of the same fabric, but it should be quilted as one large piece. However, if a block is composed of several different fabrics, as in the different parts of the Yuletide Bell, separate each fabric color by quilting in the ditch around each one.

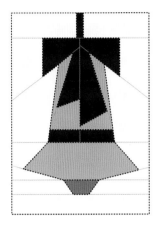

In-the-Ditch Quilting

Quilt the block background—or not. These areas may or may not be quilted. Either choice is appropriate, depending on such factors as the batting used, the projected usage of the quilt, as well as the skill of the quilter. In many projects in this book, the background areas of smaller blocks are unquilted, while the backgrounds of the larger characters are frequently stipple quilted to provide more texture and dimension. The backgrounds for Santa and Mrs. Claus in "Good Night…Sweet Dreams" were quilted using a diamond grid of parallel lines. The snowman blocks have a combination of stipple quilting in the sky area, with no quilting in the snow-covered ground area. All choices are appropriate. Consider what you like and choose accordingly.

Quilt the borders and sashings. These areas often provide ample opportunities to show off your quilting skills. Appropriate options include simple parallel lines, following the printed designs on the fabric, and the use of commercially available stencil patterns. Consider also the season and choose more personal and elaborate quilting designs that emphasize the holidays. This might include rows of quilted Christmas trees, strings of Christmas lights, holly leaves and berries, and even quilted holiday messages such as "Merry Christmas and Happy New Year."

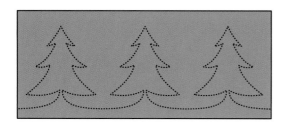

Quilter's Alert

If you decide to quilt an elaborate or seasonal design, consider using a thread color that stands out from the fabric so that your quilting stitches and the design will show up.

ATTACHING A ROD POCKET

As these quilts will frequently be hung on a wall for display, attach a rod pocket or hanging sleeve by following these steps.

1. Measure the width of your quilt at the top and subtract 2". Cut a fabric strip to that length and 5" to 9" wide, depending upon the rod you plan to use for hanging. If needed, cut more than one strip and sew the ends together to create the desired length.

2. Press under each end ¼". Press under again and stitch ⅛" from the first folded edge.

3. Fold the strip in half lengthwise, wrong sides together. Pin together at the ends and at several points in between. Press.

4. Center the rod pocket on the back of the quilt at the upper edge, aligning raw edges; pin in place. As you add the binding to the upper edge of the quilt, you will automatically attach the rod pocket.

5. After you apply the binding, hand stitch the bottom edge of the rod pocket to the quilt back. Be sure to catch only the backing and batting and leave the ends of the sleeve open, sewing only the bottom layer of the rod pocket to the quilt.

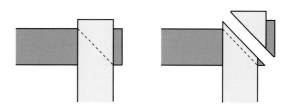

BINDING

I recommend a straight-grain, double-fold binding with mitered corners. I like binding to finish at ¼". Follow these steps to create a straight-grain, double-fold binding that will be neat and tight, with hidden ends.

1. Square up the quilt layers by trimming the excess batting and backing even with the top.

2. Using your rotary-cutting equipment, cut enough 2"-wide strips to go around the quilt, with about 12" extra for turning corners and joining the ends. Join the strips into one long continuous binding strip using diagonal seams. Press the seams open.

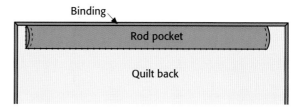

3. Press the binding in half lengthwise, wrong sides together and raw edges even.

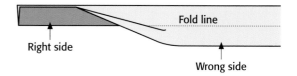

4. Starting on one side and leaving an 8" tail at the beginning, place the binding on the quilt top, aligning the raw edges of the binding with the raw edge of the quilt. Using a ¼" seam allowance, stitch the binding to the quilt top, stopping ¼" from the first corner. Backstitch and remove the quilt from the sewing machine.

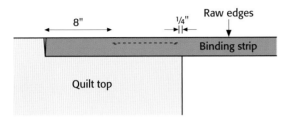

5. With the corner directly in front of you, fold the binding straight up, creating a 45° angle. Then fold the binding straight down, with the fold even with the edges of the quilt. The raw edges of the binding are now even with the next side.

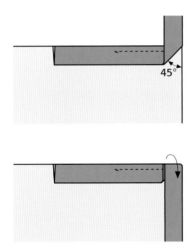

6. Begin stitching just off the fabric at the corner. The new seam is now perpendicular to the previously stitched line. Continue until you are ¼" from the next corner and repeat step 5. Repeat for each corner of the quilt, stopping 5" to 10" from where you originally began stitching. Backstitch.

7. Remove the quilt from the machine and leave an 8"-long tail of binding. Lay the quilt flat on the ironing board and carefully fold the two tails together at the center. Press, creating easily seen creases.

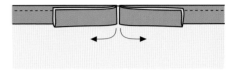

8. Unfold the strip ends. Lay one flat, with the right side up. Lay the other, right side down, over it, matching the crease points on the edges. Carefully draw a diagonal line through the point where the fold lines meet. Stitch through the marked line.

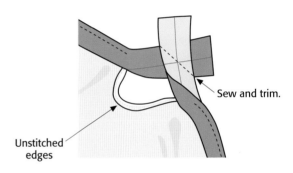

9. Check to make sure the newly attached binding is the correct length and closes the gap. If so, trim the tails off ¼" from the seam. Finger-press the seam allowance open. Refold the binding and finish sewing the binding between the beginning and ending points.

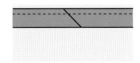

10. Gently bring the binding from the front of the quilt to the back and pin it in place. The binding should easily fold over the seam allowance and just cover the stitching line. Using a thread color that matches the binding, whipstitch the folded edge of the binding to the back of the quilt, being careful that your stitches do not go through to the front of the quilt. As you reach the corners, gently pull

the binding straight out. With your thumbnail in the corner, fold over the unstitched binding edge, creating a mitered corner. Secure it with stitching. Do this for all the corners of the quilt.

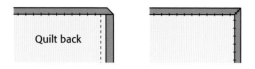

Quilt back

"Christmas Card" Labels

For these quilts and wall hangings, let your labels become a "Christmas card" to accompany each project. Provide such information as the title of the quilt, the date completed, and your name and hometown, but also include some interesting tidbits that tell a more complete story of the quilt. This might include the quilt

dimensions, any special techniques used (i.e., paper foundation piecing, machine embroidery, etc.), the source of the pattern, or the inspiration for the quilt.

Make each label a special Christmas delight by adding holiday remarks and messages, verses from holiday songs and hymns, personal wishes and dreams for the season and all year long. Share a Christmas memory. Pass on a tradition.

I have included a possible Christmas card message for each of the quilts. The phrases in red at the end of the project-photo captions are those that I used on the labels of my quilts. Feel free to use them as they are, modify them, or create your own. The main purpose is to spread holiday cheer and celebrate the Christmas season.

The Blocks and Quilts

𝒯HIS COLLECTION OF BLOCKS FEATURES IMAGES designed to "appeal to the senses" of the Yuletide season. My hope is that they call forth pleasant memories of holidays past and help you create beautiful quilts for the future.

There are 16 original blocks. Some are familiar characters of the season: Santa and Mrs. Claus, the nutcracker and toy soldier, an angel, a snowman, and a gingerbread boy and girl. Next, you will find the toys and trinkets of Christmas: rocking horses, bows, bells, stars, ornaments, and pine trees. And there are two special holiday symbols: a winter cottage gingerbread house and a feather tree.

Christmas Delights presents these Christmas characters and trinkets in a variety of quilt settings, from small one-block wall hangings, to medium-size wall quilts and throws, to larger-size bed quilts. There are very easy blocks with simple piecing and straightforward settings for beginners along with more complex blocks and multiple pieced borders for the more experienced quilter.

Throughout the book, I have emphasized Yuletide wishes and written messages. I included a casual-style alphabet and numerals (pages 92–94) so that the messages may be created on your quilts. Use them for your own personal wishes, as well. Simply enlarge or reduce the letters and numbers as desired. Let your quilts set a delightful Christmas mood, create warm memories, and tell their own unique stories.

My Christmas wishes for all of you . . .

May the Yuletide season and the patterns and designs in this book be an inspiration and a motivation for you to create your very own special Christmas quilts.

May they provide you with much holiday anticipation and excitement that electrifies your senses.

May the hours spent creating them give you peaceful moments of Christmas recollections and Yuletide remembering.

May the making of these quilts also inspire some holiday hustle and bustle as the day fast approaches and preparation time dwindles.

May these quilts help you keep the Christmas spirit and be a part of your future Christmas Delights!

Merry Christmas and Happy Holidays always!

Jaynette Huff

Radiant Angel

Block size: 9" x 15"
See foundation pattern on page 91
and pullout page 2A.

Angels are integral to Christmas. They appear atop the Christmas tree. They are the subject of hymns and Christmas carols that we sing. And many a child has aspired to be an angel in the traditional Christmas pageant. Construct this angel with outspread wings to be the focal point of your holiday quilts and wall hangings. Make one for a small wall quilt, or make "multitudes of angels" all in a row.

FABRIC KEY AND MATERIALS

Letter	Used For	Size of Fabric Needed
BK	Background	11" x 22"
D	Dress	11" x 14"
F	Flesh	6" x 6"
G	Gold halo	2" x 2"
H	Hair	5" x 5"
W1	Wing 1	6" x 11"
W2	Wing 2	6" x 11"

EMBELLISHMENTS

Tiny buttons, ¼" diameter, or beads for dress

SEWING ORDER

Part A: 1–5
Part B: 1–5
Part C: 1–5
Part D: 1–8
Join C to D (CD)
Join B to CD (BCD)
Join A to BCD (ABCD)

Part E: 1–4
Part F: 1–4
Join E to F (EF)
Join ABCD to EF (ABCDEF)
Part G: 1–4
Part H: 1–2
Join G to H (GH)
Part I: 1–4

Join GH to I (GHI)
Part J: 1–4
Part K: 1–2
Join J to K (JK)
Join GHI to JK (GHIJK)
Join ABCDEF to GHIJK
(ABCDEFGHIJK)

What captures the spirit of the Christmas season better than the spicy aroma of fresh gingerbread baking in the oven? Can't you just taste the cinnamon candies, the colored sugar sprinkles, and the sweet vanilla frosting? Now create your own fantasy figures with these 4" x 5" blocks of the Gingerbread Boy and Girl. And, the best part is: these cookies have no calories to count! Enjoy.

Block sizes: 4" x 5"
See foundation patterns on pullout page 1B.

FABRIC KEY AND MATERIALS

For either Gingerbread Boy or Gingerbread Girl

Letter	Used For	Size of Fabric Needed
BK	Background	8" x 11"
G	Gingerbread	5" x 11"

EMBELLISHMENTS

Buttons, beads, rickrack, ribbon, whatever your heart desires!

SEWING ORDER

Gingerbread Girl

Part A: 1–6
Part B: 1–5
Part C: 1–5
Join B to C (BC)
Join A to BC (ABC)
Part D: 1–3

Join ABC to D (ABCD)
Part E: 1–6
Join ABCD to E (ABCDE)

Gingerbread Boy

Part A: 1–6
Part B: 1–4
Part C: 1–6

Join B to C (BC)
Part D: 1–4
Part E: 1–6
Join D to E (DE)
Join BC to DE (BCDE)
Join A to BCDE (ABCDE)

Mrs. Claus

Block size: 14" x 23"

See foundation pattern on pullout page 1B.

What a joy to have Mrs. Claus in the house! Can't you just smell the pie and feel the warmth already? May Yuletide happiness surround you!

FABRIC KEY AND MATERIALS

Letter	Used For	Size of Fabric Needed
A	Apron	11" x 14"
AS	Apron sleeve	8" x 8"
B	Blouse	8" x 8"
BK	Background	⅓ yard
D	Dress	11" x 12"
F	Flesh	6" x 6"
P	Pie	2" x 5"
PT	Pie tin	2" x 5"
S	Shoes	4" x 4"
T	Trim on dress	7" x 6"
US	Under sleeve	3" x 3"

EMBELLISHMENTS

Embroidery floss for eyes, lips, cheeks, and outlines

SEWING ORDER

Part A: 1
Part B: 1
Part C: 1
Part D: 1–4
Part E: 1–4
Join D to E (DE)
Join C to DE (CDE)
Part F: 1–6
Part G: 1–4
Join F to G (FG)
Part H: 1–6
Join FG to H (FGH)
Join CDE to FGH (CDEFGH)
Part I: 1–5
Join CDEFGH to I (CDEFGHI)
Part J: 1–5
Part K: 1–5

Join J to K (JK)
Part L: 1–7
Part M: 1–7
Join L to M (LM)
Join JK to LM (JKLM)*
Part N: 1–5
Part O: 1–5
Join N to O (NO)
Join JKLM to NO (JKLMNO)*
Join CDEFGHI to JKLMNO (CDEFGHIJKLMNO)
Part P: 1
Part Q: 1–3
Part R: 1–6
Join Q to R (QR)
Join P to QR (PQR)
Part S: 1–3
Join PQR to S (PQRS)

Part T: 1–6
Part U: 1–3
Join T to U (TU)
Part V: 1
Join TU to V (TUV)
Join PQRS to TUV (PQRSTUV)
Part W: 1
Join PQRSTUV to W (PQRSTUVW)
Join CDEFGHIJKLMNO to PQRSTUVW (CDEFGHIJKL MNOPQRSTUVW)
Join B to CDEFGHIJKLMNO PQRSTUVW (BCDEFGHIJKL MNOPQRSTUVW)
Join A to BCDEFGHIJKLMNO PQRSTUVW (ABCDEFGHIJ KLMNOPQRSTUVW)

Leave the seam allowance free at this intersection. These points (indicated by the circles on the patterns) are pivotal points that require that the stitching stop where the stitch lines of the different parts meet. Do not stitch into the ¼" seam allowance. This allows for increased flexibility when fitting the parts together and for permitting the fabrics to lie flat.

Block size: 10" x 27"

See foundation pattern on pullout page 1A.

This brightly colored nutcracker will boost Yuletide spirits wherever he is displayed. His presence will surely bring back memories of happy holidays past.

FABRIC KEY AND MATERIALS

Letter	Used For	Size of Fabric Needed
B	Belt, boots, eyebrows, and lips	7" x 11"
BK	Background	⅓ yard
E	Eye	2" x 2"
F	Flesh	5" x 11"
H	Hair	5" x 11"
J	Jacket	11" x 15"
P	Pants	11" x 14"
T	Trim	6" x 11"
W	White teeth	3" x 3"

EMBELLISHMENTS

10 buttons, ¼" to ⅜" diameter, for jacket
Belt buckle
Embroidery floss for jacket couching
Gold cording for jacket couching
Appliquéd mustache and beard

SEWING ORDER

Part A: 1–6
Part B: 1–4
Join A to B (AB)
Part C: 1–4
Join AB to C (ABC)
Part D: 1
Part E: 1
Part F: 1–7
Part G: 1–6
Join F to G (FG)
Part H: 1–2
Part I: 1–2
Part J: 1–2
Join I to J (IJ)
Join H to IJ (HIJ)
Join FG to HIJ (FGHIJ)
Part K: 1–7

Part L: 1–6
Join K to L (KL)
Join FGHIJ to KL (FGHIJKL)
Part M: 1–9
Part N: 1–8
Join M to N (MN)
Join FGHIJKL to MN
   (FGHIJKLMN)
Join E to FGHIJKLMN
   (EFGHIJKLMN)
Join D to EFGHIJKLMN
   (DEFGHIJKLMN)
Join ABC to DEFGHIJKLMN
   (ABCDEFGHIJKLMN)
Part O: 1–2
Part P: 1–7
Part Q: 1–8

Part R: 1–7
Join Q to R (QR)
Join P to QR (PQR)
Join O to PQR (OPQR)
Part S: 1–2
Join OPQR to S (OPQRS)
Join ABCDEFGHIJKLMN to
   OPQRS (ABCDEFGHIJ
   KLMNOPQRS)
Part T: 1–3
Join ABCDEFGHIJKLMNOPQRS
   to T (ABCDEFGHIJKLMN
   OPQRST)
Part U: 1–18
Join ABCDEFGHIJKLMNOPQ
   RST to U (ABCDEFGHIJKL
   MNOPQRSTU)

Santa Claus

Block size: 14" x 23"
See foundation pattern on pullout page 2B.

Here he is, the man of the hour! But, wait, he's not in his usual attire—he's dressed in his union suit and slippers! Even Santa needs a rest sometime!

FABRIC KEY AND MATERIALS

Letter	Used For	Size of Fabric Needed
B	Beard	6" x 9"
BK	Background	⅜ yard
C	Cuffs	9" x 11"
F1	Flesh 1	9" x 11"
F2	Flesh 2	(reverse side of Flesh 1)
LJ	Long johns	11" x 22"
S	Shoe soles	6" x 6"
SL	Slippers	7" x 7"

EMBELLISHMENTS

6 buttons, ¼" diameter, for long johns
Button, ⅞" diameter, or bell for cap tassel
Appliquéd mustache
Embroidery floss for eyes, nose, cheeks, and hands

SEWING ORDER

Part A: 1
Part B: 1–8
Part C: 1–7
Join B to C (BC)
Join A to BC (ABC)
Part D: 1–5
Join ABC to D (ABCD)
Part E: 1–5
Part F: 1–5
Join E to F (EF)

Join ABCD to EF (ABCDEF)
Part G: 1–7
Join ABCDEF to G (ABCDEFG)
Part H: 1–3
Join ABCDEFG to H (ABCDEFGH)
Part I: 1–4
Part J: 1–5
Join I to J (IJ)
Part K: 1–14
Join IJ to K (IJK)
Part L: 1–4

Part M: 1–5
Join L to M (LM)
Join IJK to LM (IJKLM)
Join ABCDEFGH to IJKLM (ABCDEFGHIJKLM)
Part N: 1–13
Join ABCDEFGHIJKLM to N (ABCDEFGHIJKLMN)
Part O: 1–4
Join ABCDEFGHIJKLMN to O (ABCDEFGHIJKLMNO)

Lawrence Russell, Yuletide Snowman

Block size: 10" x 14"
See foundation pattern on pages 88–90.

When the snowflakes begin to fall, children immediately begin dreaming about snowmen! Let your imagination soar as you stitch up this frosty Yuletide character. His real counterpart may be cold to the touch, but this guy will always warm the heart!

FABRIC KEY AND MATERIALS

Letter	Used For	Size of Fabric Needed
BK	Background sky	12" x 22"
GR	Ground snow	8" x 11"
H	Hat	6" x 7"
M	Mittens	6" x 6"
S	Snowman	9" x 11"
T	Trim	7" x 6" for trim and trim reversed
Tr	Trim reversed	

EMBELLISHMENTS

4 to 6 buttons, ⅜" diameter, for snowman front
Beads or tiny buttons for eyes
Appliquéd stick arms
Embroidery floss for nose, mouth, and outlining

SEWING ORDER

Part A: 1
Part B: 1–2
Part C: 1–5
Join B to C (BC)
Part D: 1–2
Join BC to D (BCD)
Join A to BCD (ABCD)
Part E: 1–7

Part F: 1–11
Join E to F (EF)
Part G: 1–3
Join EF to G (EFG)
Join ABCD to EFG (ABCDEFG)
Part H: 1–6
Part I: 1–6
Join H to I (HI)
Part J: 1–4

Part K: 1–7
Join J to K (JK)
Join HI to JK (HIJK)
Part L: 1–3
Part M: 1–6
Join L to M (LM)
Join HIJK to LM (HIJKLM)
Join ABCDEFG to HIJKLM
    (ABCDEFGHIJKLM)

Edgar, the Friendly Toy Soldier

Block size: 10" x 27"

See foundation pattern on pullout page 1A.

Make this friendly toy soldier so he can stand guard over all your celebrations this year. He is sure to bring lots of bright smiles to the faces of all your friends and guests. Let the drumrolls begin!

FABRIC KEY AND MATERIALS

Letter	Used For	Size of Fabric Needed
B	Black hat, boots	9" x 11"
BK	Background	⅓ yard
F	Flesh	5" x 11"
G	Gold trim	6" x 11"
J	Jacket	9" x 11"
T	Tan facial features	4" x 4"
W	White pants, belt	9" x 11"

EMBELLISHMENTS

2 buttons, ⅜" to ½" diameter, for eyes
6 buttons, ⅜" to ½" diameter, for jacket
Appliquéd mustache

SEWING ORDER

Part A: 1–6
Part B: 1–4
Join A to B (AB)
Part C: 1–6
Join AB to C (ABC)
Part D: 1–2
Part E: 1–5
Join D to E (DE)
Part F: 1–2
Join DE to F (DEF)
Part G: 1–2
Part H: 1–5
Join G to H (GH)
Join DEF to GH (DEFGH)
Join ABC to DEFGH (ABCDEFGH)
Part I: 1–4
Part J: 1

Part K: 1–3
Part L: 1–3
Join K to L (KL)
Part M: 1–3
Join KL to M (KLM)
Join J to KLM (JKLM)
Join I to JKLM (IJKLM)
Part N: 1–4
Join IJKLM to N (IJKLMN)
Join ABCDEFGH to IJKLMN (ABCDEFGHIJKLMN)
Part O: 1–4
Part P: 1–3
Join O to P (OP)
Part Q: 1–4
Join OP to Q (OPQ)
Join ABCDEFGHIJKLMN to OPQ (ABCDEFGHIJKLMNOPQ)
Part R: 1–6

Part S: 1–6
Join R to S (RS)
Part T: 1–6
Join RS to T (RST)
Join ABCDEFGHIJKLMNOPQ to RST (ABCDEFGHIJKLMN OPQRST)
Part U: 1–6
Join ABCDEFGHIJKLMNO PQRST to U (ABCDEFGHI JKLMNOPQRSTU)
Part V: 1–5
Part W: 1–3
Join V to W (VW)
Join ABCDEFGHIJKLMNOP QRSTU to VW (ABCDE FGHIJKLMNOPQRSTUVW)

Yuletide Bell

Block size: 5" x 7"
See foundation pattern on pullout page 1B.

Ring in the holiday season with a golden Yuletide bell tied up with brightly colored ribbons. Let the sound of bells call forth holiday cheer and musical joy!

FABRIC KEY AND MATERIALS

Letter	Used For	Size of Fabric Needed
B	Bell	4" x 11"
BK	Background	11" x 14"
C	Clapper	2" x 2"
R	Ribbon	6" x 11"

EMBELLISHMENTS

1 button, ⅜" diameter, for bell clapper

SEWING ORDER

Part A: 1–4
Part B: 1–5
Join A to B (AB)
Part C: 1–5

Part D: 1–2
Join C to D (CD)
Part E: 1–5
Part F: 1–2
Join E to F (EF)

Join CD to EF (CDEF)
Join AB to CDEF (ABCDEF)
Part G: 1–3
Join ABCDEF to G (ABCDEFG)

Block size: 5" x 7"
See foundation pattern on pullout page 1B.

What else says "celebrate" better than pretty packages tied up with beautiful bows? This bow certainly won't be torn off and discarded, but rather, can be created and displayed for any special celebration. Place this bow in the corners of your quilt, or simply line up several all in a row.

FABRIC KEY AND MATERIALS

Letter	Used For	Size of Fabric Needed
B	Bow	9" x 11"
BK	Background	10" x 11"

EMBELLISHMENTS

1 button, ¾" diameter, for center of bow

SEWING ORDER

Part A: 1	Join B to C (BC)	Part E: 1–6
Part B: 1–7	Join A to BC (ABC)	Join D to E (DE)
Part C: 1–7	Part D: 1–5	Join ABC to DE (ABCDE)

Yuletide Ornament

Block size: 4" x 4"
See foundation pattern on page 89.

*H*ow very bare our Christmas trees would be without beautiful ornaments hung among the branches. Make these fabric Yuletide ornaments bright and colorful, add rows of silver and gold, and adorn all your holiday quilts and wall hangings.

FABRIC KEY AND MATERIALS

Letter	Used For	Size of Fabric Needed
BK	Background	5" x 11"
C1	Ornament color 1*	4" x 11"
C2	Ornament color 2*	6" x 6"
C3	Ornament color 3*	6" x 6"
G	Gold hanger	2" x 2"

For best results, choose 3 contrasting colors for C1, C2, and C3.

SEWING ORDER

Part A: 1–26
Part B: 1–4
Join A to B (AB)

Christmas Pine Tree

Block size: 5" x 7"
See foundation pattern on pullout page 1B.

Here's a Pine Tree block for almost instant holiday charm. Line up several in a row to create a wintry grove of pine trees, place one in each corner of a quilt, or heavily embellish just one for a special nook that needs a bit of Yuletide sparkle. Can't you smell the pungent aroma of fresh pine needles?

FABRIC KEY AND MATERIALS

Letter	Used For	Size of Fabric Needed
BK	Background	10" x 11"
G	Green tree	5" x 11"
T	Tree trunk	2" x 2"

EMBELLISHMENTS

Buttons, charms, beads, threads, trinkets

SEWING ORDER
Part A: 1–14

Rocking Horse

Block size: 7" x 6"
See foundation pattern on pullout page 1B.

Nothing brings a gleam to the eye and a smile to the face of a small child like climbing onto the back of his or her very own rocking horse. Let this fabric rocking horse ride into the heart of a special child in your life.

FABRIC KEY AND MATERIALS

Letter	Used For	Size of Fabric Needed
B	Blanket	5" x 5"
BK	Background	11" x 11"
H	Horse	4" x 11"
R	Rocker	3" x 6"
S	Saddle	4" x 4"
T	Tail	4" x 4"

EMBELLISHMENTS

Embroidery floss for couched mane. (Refer to page 15 for details.)

1 button, ⅜" diameter, for stirrup

1 button, ¼" diameter, for eye

SEWING ORDER

Part A: 1
Part B: 1–2
Part C: 1–4
Join B to C (BC)
Join A to BC (ABC)
Part D: 1–4
Part E: 1–5

Join D to E (DE)
Part F: 1–6
Part G: 1–2
Part H: 1
Part I: 1
Part J: 1–6
Part K: 1–6
Join J to K (JK)

Join I to JK (IJK)
Join H to IJK (HIJK)
Join G to HIJK (GHIJK)
Join F to GHIJK (FGHIJK)
Join DE to FGHIJK (DEFGHIJK)
Join ABC to DEFGHIJK
(ABCDEFGHIJK)

From the sky above to the tip-top of the Christmas tree, nothing leads the way to the holidays like a star. This 4" x 4" Star block will add sparkle to your Christmas quilts and wall hangings.

Block size: 4" x 4"
See foundation pattern on page 89.

FABRIC KEY AND MATERIALS

Letter	Used For	Size of Fabric Needed
BK	Background	5" x 11"
S	Star	6" x 6"

SEWING ORDER

Part A: 1–3
Part B: 1–3
Join A to B (AB)
Part C: 1–3
Join AB to C (ABC)

Feather Tree

Block size: 16" x 24"

See foundation pattern on pullout pages 2A and 2B.

Here's a tree that's simple and straightforward to stitch but looks complex and refined when complete. It can be used as a wonderful Advent calendar and is a great opportunity for decorating and celebrating—all the way up to Christmas Day! The kids will love to help with the holiday countdown!

FABRIC KEY AND MATERIALS

Letter	Used For	Size of Fabric Needed
BK	Background	½ yard
P	Planter	7" x 11"
T	Tree	¼ yard

EMBELLISHMENTS

24 buttons, ½" diameter, for hanging ornaments

24 miniature ornaments

1 treetop ornament (I suggest a brass or gold star.)

8 yards of ⅛"-wide ribbon for tying ornaments onto buttons

SEWING ORDER

Part A: 1–7

Part B: 1–15

Part C: 1–13

Join B to C (BC)

Join A to BC (ABC)

❧ Winter Cottage ❧

Block size: 12" x 12"
See foundation pattern on pullout page 2A.

Stitch up a cozy winter cottage where visitors are always welcome, especially during the Christmas season. This charming scene will encourage your guests to come on in, sit awhile, relax, and enjoy the holidays!

FABRIC KEY AND MATERIALS

Letter	Used For	Size of Fabric Needed
BK	Background sky	9" x 22"
C	Chimney and door	6" x 6"
H	House	9" x 11"
P	Pine tree	5" x 11"
SN1	Snow 1 and roof	6" x 22"
SN2	Snow 2	9" x 11"
SW	Sidewalk	6" x 6"
T	Trim	9" x 11"
TR	Tree trunk	2" x 2"
W	Windows	9" x 11"

EMBELLISHMENTS

1 button, ⅜" diameter, for door handle
Miniature wreath ornament for window (optional)

SEWING ORDER

Part A: 1–4
Part B: 1–4
Join A to B (AB)
Part C: 1–4
Part D: 1–3
Join C to D (CD)
Part E: 1–2
Part F: 1–3
Join E to F (EF)
Join CD to EF (CDEF)
Part G: 1–5
Join CDEF to G (CDEFG)
Part H: 1–2
Part I: 1–3
Part J: 1–3

Part K: 1–3
Part L: 1–3
Join K to L (KL)
Part M: 1–3
Join KL to M (KLM)
Part N: 1
Part O: 1–8
Part P: 1–7
Join O to P (OP)
Join N to OP (NOP)
Part Q: 1–2
Part R: 1–11
Join Q to R (QR)
Part S: 1
Part T: 1–5
Part U: 1–5

Join T to U (TU)
Join S to TU (STU)
Join QR to STU (QRSTU)
Join NOP to QRSTU (NOPQRSTU)
Join KLM to NOPQRSTU
    (KLMNOPQRSTU)
Join J to KLMNOPQRSTU
    (JKLMNOPQRSTU)
Join I to JKLMNOPQRSTU
    (IJKLMNOPQRSTU)
Join H to IJKLMNOPQRSTU
    (HIJKLMNOPQRSTU)
Join CDEFG to HIJKLMNOPQRSTU
    (CDEFGHIJKLMNOPQRSTU)
Join AB to CDEFGHIJKLMNOPQRSTU
    (ABCDEFGHIJKLMNOPQRSTU)

Quilt size: 48" x 66"

One of the most memorable sensations of the holiday season is the taste and aroma of homemade cookies fresh from the oven. And what could be more perfect than decorated gingerbread boys and girls? Sew up this quilt with Mrs. Santa Claus at its center with a freshly baked pie; encircle her with highly embellished gingerbread cookies dancing all around.

"May your Yuletide celebrations be homemade and heart-warmed!"

MATERIALS: 42"-wide fabric

Note that the borders are numbered from the center out, beginning with the narrow border around Mrs. Claus. The pieced gingerbread border is border 2.

1¾ yards for outer border 5

1⅜ yards for block background

1 yard of dark fabric for the pieced gingerbread border, Four Patch blocks, and binding

⅝ yard for borders 1 and 3, and sashing

⅝ yard for border 4

½ yard *each* of 2 different light fabrics for the pieced gingerbread border

¼ yard *each* of 3 different browns for gingerbread boys and girls (I suggest a medium-light brown, a medium brown, and a medium-dark brown)

¼ yard for message panels

¼ yard for outer-border Four Patch blocks (second color)

11" x 14" for Mrs. Claus's apron

11" x 12" for Mrs. Claus's dress

8" x 8" for Mrs. Claus's blouse

8" x 8" for Mrs. Claus's apron sleeve

Assorted scraps for Mrs. Claus's under-sleeve, trim, flesh, pie, pie tin, and shoes

4¼ yards for backing and rod pocket

54" x 72" piece of batting

Lots and lots of buttons and beads for cookie embellishments

Embroidery floss for facial features

Fabric for lettering of message

Template plastic

CUTTING

From the borders 1 and 3 and sashing fabric, cut:

    10 strips, 1½" x 42"; crosscut 6 into:

        2 strips, 1½" x 14½"

        2 strips, 1½" x 28½"

        2 strips, 1½" x 16½"

        2 strips, 1½" x 34½"

From the message panel fabric, cut:

    2 strips, 3" x 14½"

From the dark fabric for the pieced gingerbread border, Four Patch blocks, and binding, cut:

    2 strips, 3¼" x 42"

    3 strips, 2¾" x 42"

    1 strip, 3" x 42"; crosscut into:

        8 squares, 3" x 3"

    6 strips, 2" x 42", for binding

From each of the light fabrics for the pieced gingerbread border, cut:

    3 strips, 4¾" x 42"

From the border 4 fabric, cut:

    6 strips, 2½" x 42"

From the second four-patch fabric, cut:

    1 strip, 3" x 42"; crosscut into:

        8 squares, 3" x 3"

From the outer border 5 fabric, cut on the lengthwise grain:

    4 strips, 5½" x 63"

ASSEMBLY

1. Using the foundation pattern for Mrs. Claus on pullout page 1B, trace one pattern onto freezer paper.

2. Make templates from template plastic using patterns A, B, and C on page 95.

3. Refer to "Successful Paper Foundation Piecing" on page 7 to construct the block, following the sewing order and fabric key on page 24. Trim the block to 14½" x 21½". Most of the trim should come off the top.

4. Sew the 1½" x 14½" sashing strips to the top and bottom of the Mrs. Claus block. Press seam allowances toward the sashing. Stitch the 3" x 14½" message panels to the top and bottom sashing strips. Press toward the sashing.

5. Stitch the 1½" x 28½" border 1 pieces to the quilt sides. Press the seam allowances toward the borders. Stitch the 1½" x 16½" border 1 pieces to the quilt top and bottom edges. Press.

6. Using the 4" x 5" foundation patterns for the Gingerbread Boy and Girl blocks on pullout page 1B, trace seven of each pattern onto freezer paper, for a total of 14 blocks.

7. Refer to "Successful Paper Foundation Piecing" on page 7 to construct the blocks, following the sewing order and fabric key for each on page 23. The blocks should measure 4½" x 5½". Construct four or five boys and girls from each of the three gingerbread fabrics, for a total of 14 blocks (7 boys and 7 girls).

8. Lay template A on the dark 3¼" x 42" strips. Trace and cut out 28 triangles, alternating the triangle direction with each cut. Repeat to cut 28 triangles using template B and the 2¾" x 42" strips.

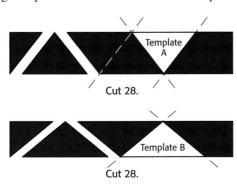

9. Stitch the template A triangles to the top and bottom of each Gingerbread Boy and Girl block. Stitch template B triangles to the sides of each block. Press the seam allowances toward the triangles. Handle the blocks gently, as the outer bias edges can stretch easily.

10. Lay template C on the 4¾" x 42" strips of one of the light fabrics. Trace and cut out 14 triangles, alternating the triangle direction with each cut. Turn the template over to the reverse side (Cr), and cut an additional 14 triangles, alternating the triangle direction with each cut.

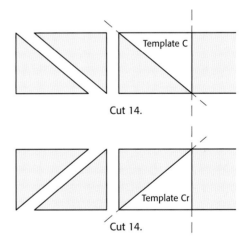

11. Repeat step 10 with the 4¾" x 42" strips of the second light fabric. Cut 14 template C triangles and 14 template Cr triangles.

12. Arrange the Gingerbread Boy and Girl blocks as shown.

13. Beginning with the gingerbread girl in the upper-right-hand corner and going in a clockwise direction, alternate the color of the C and Cr triangles with each block. Carefully stitch two template C triangles and two template Cr triangles to the corners of each block, making a rectangle 8½" x 10½". Press the seam allowances toward the template C pieces.

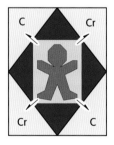

Taming Bias Edges

In step 13, you will be sewing bias edges to bias edges. Handle the blocks and triangle pieces very carefully, and pin along the edges before sewing.

14. Make two horizontal rows of four blocks each: boy, girl, boy, girl. Make sure the cookies are standing upright and the points match. Press the seam allowances open.

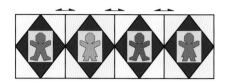

Make 2.

15. Make two vertical rows of three blocks each. One row should be girl, boy, girl. The other row should be boy, girl, boy. Make sure the cookies are standing upright and the points match. Press the seam allowances open.

Make 1.   Make 1.

16. Stitch the girl-boy-girl vertical row to the left side of the quilt. Stitch the boy-girl-boy vertical row to the right side of the quilt. Press the seam allowances open. Stitch the two horizontal block rows to the top and bottom edges of the quilt, making sure the kids are upright and the points match. Press the seam allowances open.

17. Stitch two 1½" x 42" border 3 strips together end to end to make one long strip. Make two. Measure the quilt top through the center to determine the length. Cut two pieced strips to the length measured. Stitch the strips to the quilt sides. Press the seam allowances toward the borders. Stitch the 1½" x 34½" border 3 strips to the quilt top and bottom. Press.

18. Stitch two border 4 strips together end to end to make one long strip. Make two. Measure the quilt top through the center to determine the length. Cut two pieced strips to the length measured and sew to the quilt sides. Press the seam allowances toward the borders. Measure the quilt top through the center to determine the width. Cut two border 4 strips to the width measured and stitch to the quilt top and bottom. Press.

19. Using the 3" x 3" squares, make 4 Four Patch blocks as shown for the outer border.

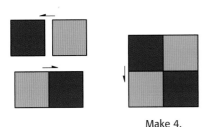

Make 4.

20. Measure the quilt top through the center to determine the length and width. Cut two outer-border 5 strips to the length measured and stitch to the quilt sides. Press toward the border strips. Cut two outer-border 5 strips to the width measured.

21. Stitch the Four Patch blocks to each end of the outer-border 5 strips, rotating the Four Patch blocks to position the colors as shown. Stitch the pieced strips to the quilt top and bottom. Press.

FINISHING THE QUILT

Refer to "Finishing" on pages 14–20.

1. Embroider the facial details and appliqué the message using the patterns on pages 92–93. The letters used are 1½" tall, so you will need to reduce the patterns by 75%. Refer to "Appliqué" on page 15 for additional details on your chosen method of appliqué.

2. Cut and piece the backing fabric vertically. Press seams open.

3. Layer the quilt top with batting and backing; baste.

4. Quilt as desired.

5. Square up the quilt top.

6. Add a rod pocket and bind the quilt.

7. Embellish with beads and buttons as desired.

8. Stitch a "Christmas card" label to the quilt back.

Quilt size: 58" x 79"

Stand up and cheer! Stand up and salute! Here come the boys of Christmas—Dudley, the Christmas nutcracker, and Edgar, the friendly toy soldier. Just look at their military uprightness, the crisp, snappy colors of their uniforms, their highly polished buttons and belt buckles! Let them welcome your guests in the entryway, stand guard over the Christmas feast in the dining room, or cover the wall of the family room.

"Hurray! Hurrah! For Christmas Day!"

MATERIALS: 42"-wide fabric

2⅝ yards for block background and inner border

2¼ yards for outer border and binding

1½ yards for sashing and outer-border corner squares

¾ yard for stars and middle-border corner squares

½ yard of black for blocks

½ yard for middle border (narrow accent border)

½ yard for nutcracker jackets

½ yard for nutcracker pants

⅜ yard for gold trim

¼ yard for toy soldier jackets

¼ yard for toy soldier pants

¼ yard for flesh

Assorted scraps for hair, eyes, teeth, beards, mustaches, and facial features

4¾ yards for backing and rod pocket

64" x 85" piece of batting

3 gold buckles

24–36 buttons, ¼" diameter, for jackets

Gold cording

6 buttons for soldiers' eyes

Template plastic

CUTTING

From the stars and middle-border–corner-squares fabric, cut:

    6 strips, 2¼" x 42"

    2 strips, 3½" x 42"; crosscut into:

        12 squares, 3½" x 3½"

    4 squares, 1½" x 1½"

From the sashing and outer-border–corner-squares fabric, cut:

    11 strips, 3½" x 42"; crosscut into:

        9 strips, 3½" x 11¼"

        8 strips, 3½" x 28¼"

    1 strip, 4" x 42"

    1 strip, 4½" x 42"; crosscut into:

        4 squares, 4½" x 4½"

From the background and inner-border fabric, cut:

    5 strips, 3½" x 42"; crosscut into:

        4 strips, 3½" x 27½"

        6 strips, 3½" x 10½"

        4 squares, 3½" x 3½"

From the middle-border fabric, cut:

    8 strips, 1½" x 42"

From the outer-border and binding fabric, cut on the lengthwise grain:

    4 strips, 4½" x 81"

    4 strips, 2" x 81", for binding

ASSEMBLY

1. Using the foundation patterns for Edgar, the Friendly Toy Soldier and Dudley, the Christmas Nutcracker on pullout page 1A, trace three of each onto freezer paper.

2. Make templates from template plastic using patterns D, E, and F on pullout page 2B.

3. Refer to "Successful Paper Foundation Piecing" on pages 7–14 to construct the blocks following the sewing order and fabric key for each on pages 25 and 28. The blocks should measure 10½" x 27½" before you add any sashing or borders. If they do not, be sure to adjust the lengths of the sashing and border strips accordingly.

4. To make the star triangle points, lay template D on the 2¼" x 42" strips. Trace and cut out 96 triangles, 48 D and 48 D reverse.

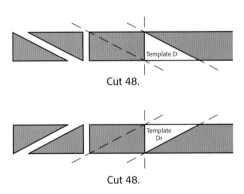

Cut 48.

Cut 48.

5. Using template F as a guide, trim off the corners of each 3½" x 11¼" sashing piece.

Trimming template F

6. Sew the D triangles to the ends of the trimmed sashing piece as shown. Press the seam allowances toward the triangles. Each unit should measure 3½" x 10½" when complete. Make nine.

Make 9.

Stitcher's Alert

For precise matching of these D and D reverse triangles with the trimmed sashing pieces, lightly draw in the sewing lines on the wrong side of each fabric piece, marking the points where the seams intersect. Then, when aligning the fabric pieces right sides together, insert a pin through each corresponding seam intersection. Ease the fabrics and pin them as needed. Then sew along the marked lines.

7. Use template F again as a guide to trim off the corners of each 3½" x 28¼" sashing strip. You can fold the strips in half to trim both ends at once. Be sure that the point of the template is touching the cut end of the fabric. Sew the D triangles to the ends as shown. Press the seam allowances toward the triangles. Each unit should measure 3½" x 27½" when complete. Make eight.

Make 8.

8. To make the sashing rows, alternately sew together four 3½" star-fabric squares and three short sashing units from step 6. Press the seam allowances toward the squares. Make three.

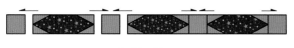

Sashing Row
Make 3.

9. To make the block rows, alternately stitch together four long sashing units and three blocks. Note the placement of the nutcrackers and toy soldiers. Press the seam allowances toward the blocks.

10. Alternating sashing and block rows, stitch the rows together. Press seam allowances toward the sashing.

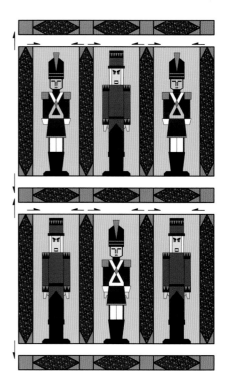

11. To make the inner border, first piece together the Star Point blocks. Using template E, trace and cut 14 E triangles from the 4"-wide strip of sashing fabric; alternate the triangle direction with each cut. Sew a D triangle and a D reverse to two sides of each E triangle. Press the seam allowances toward the D triangles. Make 14.

Make 14.

12. Sew together three Star Point blocks and two 3½" x 27½" background strips, making sure the star points are all going in the correct direction. Press the seam allowances toward the background strips. Make two. Stitch to the quilt sides, being sure to match the seam intersections. Press the seam allowances toward the sashing.

13. Make the top and bottom strips by sewing together two inner-border corner squares, four Star Point blocks, and three inner-border strips, 3½" x 10½", as shown. Press the seam allowances toward the strips and corner squares. Make two rows. Stitch to the top and bottom of the quilt, being careful to match the seam intersections. Press the seams toward the border.

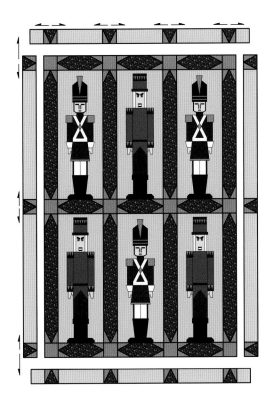

14. Stitch two middle-border strips together end to end to make one long strip. Repeat to make four. Measure the quilt top through the center to determine length and width. Cut two middle-border strips to the quilt-length measurement for the sides; cut two middle-border strips to the quilt-width measurement for the top and bottom edges. Stitch the side borders to the quilt. Press the seams toward the border.

15. Stitch the middle-border corner squares to each end of the top and bottom strips. Stitch the pieced strips to the quilt. Press toward the border strips.

16. Measure the quilt top through the center to determine length and width. Cut two 4½" outer-border strips to the quilt-length measurement for the

sides; cut two outer-border strips to the quilt-width measurement for the top and bottom edges. Stitch the side borders to the quilt sides. Press toward the border strips.

17. Stitch the outer-border corner squares to each end of the top and bottom strips. Stitch the pieced strips to the quilt. Press.

FINISHING THE QUILT

Refer to "Finishing" on pages 14–20.

1. Appliqué the mustaches and beards to each character, and couch the jacket decoration to the nutcrackers, referring to "Couching" on page 15.

2. Cut and piece the backing fabric vertically.

3. Layer the quilt top with batting and backing; baste.

4. Quilt as desired.

5. Square up the quilt top.

6. Add a rod pocket and bind the quilt.

7. Embellish with buttons and buckles as desired.

8. Stitch a "Christmas card" label to the quilt back.

Quilt size: 14" x 24"

This design is eye-catching yet simple, the construction is fast and fun, and the message is perfectly clear . . . celebrate! Whether you choose seasonal Christmas colors of red and green or go patriotic with red, white, and blue, this simple quilt of three stars arranged in a vertical row will enhance any wall space.

"Let's make it a patriotic Christmas this year!"

MATERIALS: 42"-wide fabric

⅜ yard for outer border
¼ yard for sashing
¼ yard for middle border
⅛ yard for block background
⅛ yard for inner border
3" x 14" piece of fabric for sashing corner squares
Scraps or 6" x 6" pieces of 3 different fabrics for stars
½ yard for backing and rod pocket
⅜ yard for binding
20" x 30" piece of batting

CUTTING

From the sashing fabric, cut:
    2 strips, 1½" x 42"; crosscut into:
        10 strips, 1½" x 4½"

From the sashing-corner-square fabric, cut:
    8 squares, 1½" x 1½"

From the inner-border fabric, cut:
    2 strips, ¾" x 42"; crosscut into:
        2 strips, ¾" x 16½"
        2 strips, ¾" x 7"

From the middle-border fabric, cut:
    2 strips, 1¼" x 42"; crosscut into:
        2 strips, 1¼" x 17"
        2 strips, 1¼" x 8½"

From the outer-border fabric, cut:
    2 strips, 3½" x 42"; crosscut into:
        2 strips, 3½" x 18½"
        2 strips, 3½" x 14½"

From the binding fabric, cut:
    2 strips, 2" x 42"

ASSEMBLY

1. Using the foundation pattern for the Yuletide Star block on page 89, trace three patterns onto freezer paper.

2. Refer to "Successful Paper Foundation Piecing" on pages 7–14 to construct the blocks, following the sewing order and fabric key on page 34. The blocks should measure 4½" x 4½".

3. Arrange the blocks vertically, placing the colors as desired.

4. To make the horizontal sashing rows, stitch a corner square to each end of four sashing strips. Press seams toward the sashing.

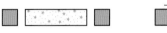 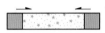

Make 4.

5. Stitch a sashing strip to the right and left side of each Star block. Press the seams toward the sashing.

 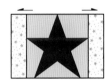

Make 3.

6. Stitch the rows together as shown. Press the seams toward the sashing.

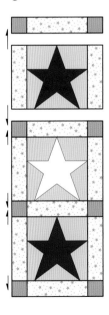

7. Sew the ¾" x 16½" inner-border strips to the quilt sides. Press the seam allowances toward the border strips. Sew the ¾" x 7" inner-border strips to the quilt top and bottom. Press.

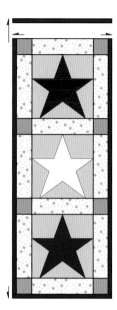

8. Repeat step 7 to attach the middle-border strips and the outer-border strips.

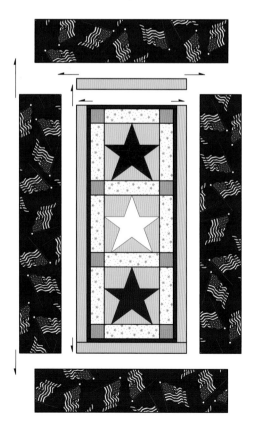

Try It!

Make this quilt and use it on your table accompanied by candlesticks and coordinating candles. Or gather all your star-shaped decorations and group them with the quilt.

FINISHING THE QUILT

Refer to "Finishing" on pages 14–20.

1. Layer the quilt top with batting and backing; baste.
2. Quilt as desired.
3. Square up the quilt top.
4. Add a rod pocket and bind the quilt.
5. Embellish with beads and buttons as desired.
6. Stitch a "Christmas card" label to the quilt back.

Dashing Ornaments
and Delightful Four Patches

Quilt size: 20" x 20"

Create this nine-block quilt of Christmas ornaments and easy Four Patch blocks. Construct each ornament with the same fabrics, or make them all different. Add interest to your Four Patch blocks with "fussy-cut" holiday motifs, or let them be wild and crazy or scrappy and homey. Whatever you choose, this quilt will add Yuletide cheer to any decor.

"May these baubles of the Christmas tree bring forth warm Yuletide memories!"

MATERIALS: 42"-wide fabric

⅜ yard for outer border and binding
¼ yard for block background
¼ yard for ornament color 1
¼ yard for inner border
⅛ yard for ornament color 2
⅛ yard for ornament color 3
⅛ yard for middle border
3" x 22" for Four Patch fabric 1
3" x 22" for Four Patch fabric 2
2" x 11" piece of gold fabric for ornament top
Scrap for outer-border corner squares
¾ yard for backing and rod pocket
24" x 24" piece of batting

CUTTING

From each of the 2 Four Patch fabrics, cut:
    8 squares, 2½" x 2½", for a total of 16 squares
From the inner-border fabric, cut:
    2 strips, 1½" x 42"; crosscut into:
        2 strips, 1½" x 12½"
        2 strips, 1½" x 14½"
From the middle-border fabric, cut:
    2 strips, 1" x 42"; crosscut into:
        2 strips, 1" x 14½"
        2 strips, 1" x 15½"
From the outer-border and binding fabric, cut:
    2 strips, 3" x 42"; crosscut into:
        4 strips, 3" x 15½"
    2 strips, 2" x 42", for binding
From the corner-square fabric, cut:
    4 squares, 3" x 3"

Ornament Collector's Alert

Pair this quilt with a bowl or basket of vintage glass ornaments on a table or sideboard.

ASSEMBLY

1. Using the foundation pattern for the Yuletide Ornament block on page 89, trace five ornament patterns.
2. Refer to "Successful Paper Foundation Piecing" on pages 7–14 to construct the blocks, following the sewing order and fabric key on page 31. The blocks should measure 4½" x 4½".
3. Stitch the 2½" x 2½" squares together as shown to create the Four Patch blocks.

Make 4.

4. Arrange the five Ornament blocks and the Four Patch blocks in three rows of three blocks each as shown. Stitch the blocks together. Press the seam allowances toward the Four Patch blocks. Sew the rows together and press toward the top and bottom rows.

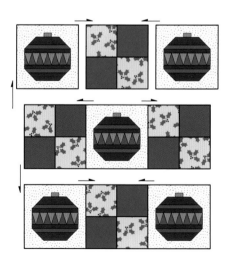

5. Sew the 1½" x 12½" inner-border strips to the quilt sides. Press the seam allowances toward the border. Sew the remaining two inner-border strips to the quilt top and bottom. Press.

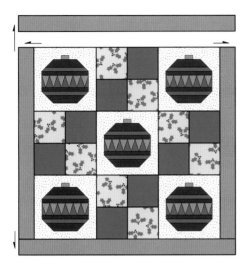

6. Repeat step 5 to add the middle-border strips to the quilt.

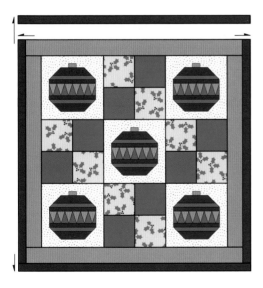

7. Sew two outer-border strips to the quilt sides. Press seams toward the outer border. Stitch the corner squares to each end of the remaining border strips. Stitch the pieced borders to the quilt top and bottom. Press.

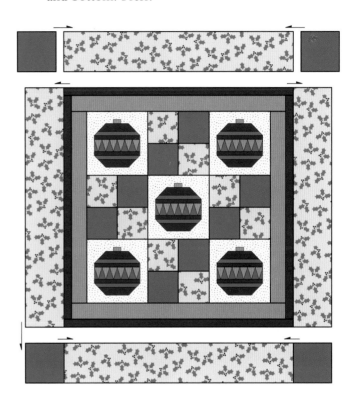

FINISHING THE QUILT

Refer to "Finishing" on pages 14–20.
1. Layer the quilt top with batting and backing; baste.
2. Quilt as desired.
3. Square up the quilt top.
4. Add a rod pocket and bind the quilt.
5. Embellish as desired.
6. Stitch a "Christmas card" label to the quilt back.

Edgar, the Friendly Toy Soldier

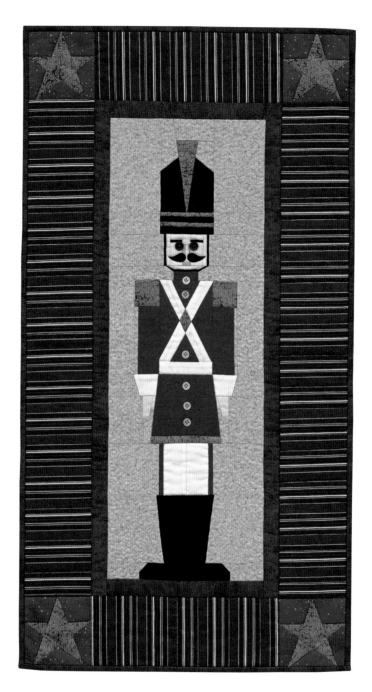

Quilt size: 19½" x 37"

Countless children have enjoyed hours of fun playing with whole armies of tiny toy soldiers: standing them in opposing lines, arranging them in perfectly straight columns; toppling them over as the enemy advances, and making the sounds of battle with trumpets blaring and horses neighing. But this toy soldier is a friendly fellow who is just looking for a place to call home. Why not invite him in to stand guard over all your Yuletide festivities?

"May your path be paved with stars."

MATERIALS: 42"-wide fabric

½ yard for inner border and binding
½ yard for outer border
⅜ yard for block background
¼ yard for star-block background
⅛ yard for stars
Assorted scraps for black, gold trim, jacket, white,
    flesh, mustache, and tan for facial features
1 yard for backing and rod pocket
26" x 43" piece of batting
2 buttons, ⅜" to ½" diameter, for eyes
6 buttons, ⅜" to ½" diameter, for jacket

CUTTING

From the inner-border and binding fabric, cut:
    2 strips, 1½" x 42"; crosscut into:
        2 strips, 1½" x 10"
        2 strips, 1½" x 29½"
    3 strips, 2" x 42", for binding
From the outer-border fabric, cut:
    3 strips, 4½" x 42"; crosscut into:
        2 strips, 4½" x 12"
        2 strips, 4½" x 29½"

Decorator's Alert

Use the toy soldier wall hanging as a backdrop for
an arrangement of vintage toys, musical instru-
ments, or antique Christmas decorations.

ASSEMBLY

1. Using the Edgar, the Friendly Toy Soldier foundation pattern on pullout page 1A, trace one pattern
   onto freezer paper.
2. Using the 4" x 4" foundation pattern for the
   Yuletide Star block on page 89, trace four star patterns onto freezer paper.
3. Refer to "Successful Paper Foundation Piecing" on
   pages 7–14 to construct the blocks, following the
   sewing order and fabric key on page 28 for the toy
   soldier, and on page 34 for the star. Using your

rotary-cutting equipment, trim the toy soldier
block to 10" x 27½", being sure to center the
figure. The Star blocks should measure 4½" x 4½".

4. Sew the 1½" x 10" inner-border strips to the top
   and bottom of the block. Press the seam
   allowances toward the border. Sew the remaining
   inner-border strips to the quilt sides. Press.
5. Sew the 4½" x 12" outer-border strips to the
   top and bottom. Press toward the outer border.
   Stitch a Star block to each end of the remaining
   4½" x 29½" outer-border strips, making sure all
   the stars are positioned the same. Press seam
   allowances toward the border strips. Stitch the
   pieced strips to the quilt sides. Press.

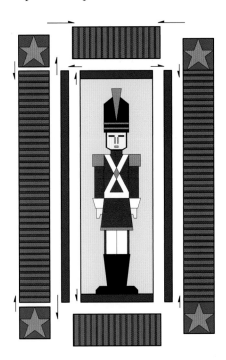

FINISHING YOUR QUILT

Refer to "Finishing" on pages 14–20.

1. Embroider and appliqué any desired block details.
2. Layer the quilt top with batting and backing; baste.
3. Quilt as desired.
4. Square up the quilt top.
5. Add a rod pocket and bind the quilt.
6. Embellish with buttons for Edgar's eyes and jacket
   front.
7. Stitch a "Christmas card" label to the quilt back.

Quilt size: 34" x 46"

We can thank our German immigrants for sharing with us the Yuletide tradition of the feather tree. Originally crafted from a wire frame and dyed goose feathers, they often were adorned with small candles, Christmas cookies, and trinkets.

This quilted feather tree showcases a collection of miniature ornaments and begins the countdown until Christmas. The calendar has 24 gold buttons sewn along the branches and around the tree; 24 more buttons are sewn around the checkerboard border, for hanging your small ornaments. Beginning on December 1, move an ornament from the border to the tree each day.

On the back of the quilt, in a small fabric pocket, is hidden the most beautiful ornament of all, one large golden star, to be hung from the treetop on Christmas morning. Hurray! Christmas Day is here!

"Count down to Christmas with great blessings!"

MATERIALS: 42"-wide fabric

1⅛ yards for block background and color 1 of the pieced checkerboard border

⅞ yard for outer border

¾ yard for inner borders 1 and 3 and binding

½ yard for Feather Tree and trees in Tree blocks

¼ yard for color 2 of the pieced checkerboard border

Assorted scraps for tree trunk, planter, and pocket on back of quilt

1¾ yards for backing and rod pocket

40" x 52" piece of batting

24 buttons, ¾" diameter, for checkerboard border

24 buttons, ½" diameter, for Feather Tree block

1 gold star for treetop

24 miniature ornaments

8 yards of ⅛"-wide ribbon for ties

Beads, buttons, and bells for corner Pine Tree blocks

CUTTING

From the inner-border and binding fabric, cut:

3 strips, 1½" x 42"; crosscut into:
    2 strips, 1½" x 24½"
    2 strips, 1½" x 18½"
4 strips, 1½" x 42"; crosscut into:
    2 strips, 1½" x 30½"
    2 strips, 1½" x 24½"
4 strips, 2" x 42", for binding

From the background and color 1 checkerboard border fabric, cut:

2 strips, 2½" x 42"; crosscut into:
    24 squares, 2½" x 2½"

From the color 2 checkerboard border fabric, cut:

2 strips, 2½" x 42"; crosscut into:
    24 squares, 2½" x 2½"

From the outer-border fabric, cut:

2 strips, 5½" x 42"
2 strips, 7½" x 42"

ASSEMBLY

1. Using the Feather Tree foundation pattern on pull-out pages 2A and 2B, trace one pattern onto freezer paper.

2. Refer to "Successful Paper Foundation Piecing" on pages 7–14 to construct the block, following the sewing order and fabric key on page 35. The block should measure 16½" x 24½".

3. Sew the 1½" x 24½" inner-border strips to the block sides. Press the seam allowances toward the border strips. Sew the 1½" x 18½" inner-border strips to the top and bottom of the block. Press.

4. To assemble the checkerboard border, stitch the 2½" x 2½" squares together, alternating the colors. For the sides, stitch together 13 squares, beginning and ending with color 1. Press seam allowances toward the darker fabric. Make two. Stitch the pieced borders to the sides of the quilt. Press the seam allowances toward the inner border.

   For the top and bottom, stitch together 11 squares, beginning and ending with color 2. Press the seams toward the darker fabric. Stitch the pieced borders to the top and bottom of the quilt. Press.

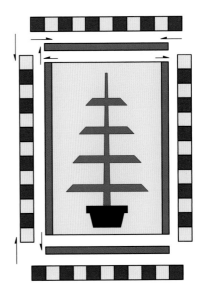

5. Stitch the 1½" x 30½" inner-border strips to the quilt sides. Press the seam allowances toward the border strips. Sew the 1½" x 24½" strips to the top and bottom of the quilt. Press.

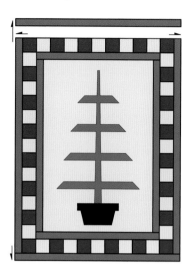

6. Using the foundation pattern for the Christmas Pine Tree block on pullout page 1B, trace four patterns onto freezer paper.

7. Construct the blocks, following the sewing order and fabric key on page 32. The blocks should measure 5½" x 7½".

8. Measure the quilt top through the center to determine its length and width. Cut the 5½"-wide outer-border strips to the length measurement and stitch the strips to the sides of the quilt. Press the seam allowances toward the outer border.

9. Cut the 7½"-wide outer-border strips to the width measurement for the top and bottom. Stitch a Pine Tree block to each end of these strips, making sure the pine trees are upright. Press seams toward

the border. Stitch the pieced border to the quilt top and bottom. Press the seam allowances toward the outer-border strips.

FINISHING YOUR QUILT

Refer to "Finishing" on pages 14–20.

1. Layer the quilt top with batting and backing; baste.
2. Quilt as desired.
3. Square up the quilt top.
4. Add a rod pocket and bind the quilt.
5. Embellish by stitching 24 buttons around the pieced checkerboard border, placing a button in the center of each color 2 block.
6. Sew 24 buttons onto the Feather Tree block, where indicated on the pattern.
7. Decorate the four Pine Tree blocks with buttons, beads, and bells.
8. Tie ribbons to each ornament and hang them on the buttons in the border.
9. Stitch a pocket to the quilt back for the special gold star ornament.
10. Stitch a "Christmas card" label to the quilt back.

Good Night . . . Sweet Dreams

Quilt size: 55" x 46½"

Place Santa and Mrs. Claus side by side and let them grace the walls of your guest room this holiday season.
Dress Santa in his favorite red long johns and clothe Mrs. Claus in her soft, warm nightgown.
She's carrying a candlestick that leads the way to peaceful slumber and pleasant dreams.

Together, let them express a loving, caring, and quiet wish for the holiday nights.
This Christmas season may we all experience "good nights and sweet dreams."

"May all your dreams this Yuletide season be sweet and happy!"

MATERIALS: 42"-wide fabric

1⅝ yards for outer border and binding

¾ yard for block background

⅝ yard for sashing

⅜ yard for inner border

¼ yard, or scraps, for sashing corner squares

⅛ yard, or scraps, for inner-border corner squares

11" x 22" for Santa's long johns

11" x 14" for Mrs. Claus's apron

11" x 12" for Mrs. Claus's nightgown

Assorted scraps for Mrs. Claus's upper nightgown, apron sleeve, under-sleeve, trim, shoes, flesh, candle, candleholder, flame, and leaves

Assorted scraps for Santa's cuffs, flesh, slippers, shoe soles, beard, and mustache

3½ yards for backing and rod pocket

61" x 53" piece of batting

Fabric for lettering of message

Embroidery floss for facial features and outlining

Buttons for Santa's long johns

Bell or button for Santa's cap

CUTTING

From the sashing fabric, cut:
> 4 strips, 4½" x 42"; crosscut into:
>> 3 strips, 4½" x 23"
>> 4 strips, 4½" x 14"

From the sashing-corner-square fabric, cut:
> 6 squares, 4½" x 4½"

From the inner-border fabric, cut:
> 2 strips, 2½" x 31"
> 2 strips, 2½" x 39½"

From the inner-border–corner-square fabric, cut:
> 4 squares, 2½" x 2½"

From the outer-border and binding fabric, cut on the lengthwise grain:
> 4 strips, 6½" x 58"
> 4 strips, 2" x 58", for binding

ASSEMBLY

1. Using the foundation pattern for Mrs. Claus on pullout page 1B and the foundation pattern for Santa on pullout page 2B, trace one of each onto freezer paper.

   Note: Be sure to change the fabric designations for part M (M4 and M5; see pattern illustration on page 59) of Mrs. Claus to reflect the candleholder and apron. M4 becomes the candleholder fabric. M5 becomes the apron fabric.

2. Refer to "Successful Paper Foundation Piecing" on pages 7–14 to construct Santa and Mrs. Claus, following the sewing order and fabric key for each block on pages 24 and 26. Trim each of the blocks to 14" x 23".

3. To make the sashing rows, alternately stitch together three sashing corner squares and two 4½" x 14" sashing strips. Press the seam allowances toward the sashing. Make two.

4. To make the block row, alternately stitch together the 4½" x 23" sashing strips and the two character blocks. Press the seam allowances toward the sashing.

5. Sew the sashing rows and the block row together. Press the seam allowances toward the sashing.

6. Sew the 2½" x 31" inner-border strips to the sides of the quilt. Press the seam allowances toward the border. Stitch the inner-border corner squares to each end of the 2½" x 39½" top and bottom strips. Stitch the pieced strips to the quilt top and bottom. Press.

7. Measure the quilt top through the center to determine the length. Cut two 6½"-wide outer-border strips to the exact measurement and stitch to the quilt sides. Press the seam allowances toward the border strips. Measure the quilt top through the center to determine the width. Cut the remaining two outer-border strips to the exact measurement and stitch the strips to the top and bottom edges of the quilt. Press the seam allowances toward the border strips.

8. **Lettering.** Use the alphabet letters provided on pages 92–93 or create your own 2" letters. Make templates; then trace the letters and cut out from fabric, adding a seam allowance if needed for your preferred appliqué method. Hand or machine appliqué them to the outer border, spacing them as desired. Refer to page 15 for appliqué instructions.

FINISHING YOUR QUILT

Refer to "Finishing" on pages 14–20.

1. Hand or machine appliqué the candle, flame, and leaves to Mrs. Claus, using the template patterns and placement guide below. Appliqué the mustache to Santa. Be sure to add seam allowance if using needle-turn appliqué.
2. Embroider block details as desired.
3. Cut the backing fabric in half and stitch the pieces together vertically.
4. Layer the quilt top with batting and backing; baste.
5. Quilt as desired.
6. Square up the quilt top.
7. Add a rod pocket and bind the quilt.
8. Embellish as desired with buttons or bell.
9. Stitch a "Christmas card" label to the quilt back.

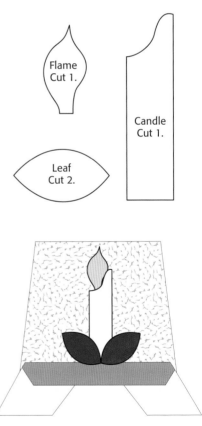

Appliqué Patterns and Placement Diagram

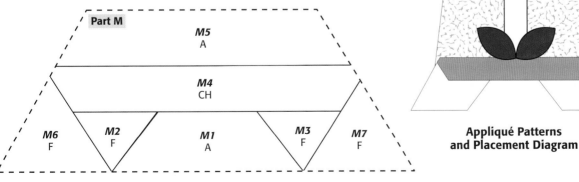

Foundation Pattern

Quilt size: 55" x 47"

Herald the season's arrival with messages of joy! Express holiday well wishes with this quilted wall hanging. Add traditional greetings such as "Merry Christmas" and "Happy New Year!" or personalize your message with family names and special thoughts. Line up these bells and let them spread the Yuletide cheer! Proclaim, "Ring Out, O' Bells! Announce the Good News!"

"Hear the bells on Christmas Day! Peace on earth, good will to all!"

MATERIALS: 42"-wide fabric

1½ yards for outer border and binding

1⅛ yards for block background 1 and message panels

⅞ yard for middle border

¾ yard for block background 2

⅝ yard for sashing

½ yard for ribbons

⅜ yard for bells

¼ yard for inner border

3 yards for backing and rod pocket

61" x 53" piece of batting

Appliqué fabric for lettering

9 buttons, ⅜" diameter, for bell clappers

9 buttons, ⅝" diameter, for center of ribbons

CUTTING

From the sashing fabric, cut:

    4 strips, 2½" x 33½"

    2 strips, 2½" x 25½"

    4 strips, 2½" x 7½"

From the block background 1 and message-panel fabric, cut:

    2 strips, 5½" x 33½"

From the inner-border fabric*, cut:

    2 strips, 1½" x 37½"

    2 strips, 1½" x 27½"

From the middle-border fabric*, cut:

    2 strips, 7½" x 39½"

    2 strips, 5½" x 27½"

From the outer-border and binding fabric*, cut on the lengthwise grain:

    2 strips, 3½" x 49½"

    2 strips, 3½" x 47½"

    4 strips, 2" x 54", for binding

* You may want to wait until the five Bell blocks and the sashing are assembled to cut the border strips.

ASSEMBLY

1. Using the Yuletide Bell foundation pattern on pullout page 1B, trace nine patterns, reversing five.

2. Refer to "Successful Paper Foundation Piecing" on pages 7–14 to construct the blocks, following the sewing order and fabric key on page 29. Make the five inner Bell blocks with block background 2 (two regular foundations and three reversed). Make the four corner Bell blocks using block background 1 (two regular and two reversed). The blocks should measure 5½" x 7½".

3. Arrange the five inner Bell blocks horizontally. Stitch together four 7½"-long vertical sashing strips and five Bell blocks. Press the seam allowances toward the sashing.

4. Stitch a 2½" x 33½" sashing strip to both the top and bottom of the quilt. Press toward the sashing.

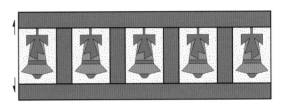

5. Stitch the 5½" x 33½" message panels to the top and bottom of the quilt. Press the seam allowances toward the sashing.

6. Stitch the remaining 2½" x 33½" sashing strips to the top and bottom. Press toward the sashing.

7. Stitch the 2½" x 25½" sashing strips to the quilt sides. Press the seams toward the sashing.

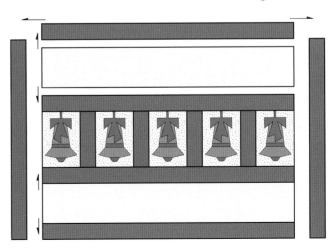

8. Measure the quilt top through the center to determine its width. Cut the 1½" x 37½" inner-border strips to the exact measurement and stitch the strips to the top and bottom. Press the seam allowances toward the darker fabric. Measure the quilt top through the center to determine its length. Cut the 1½" x 27½" inner-border strips to the exact measurement and stitch the strips to the quilt sides. Press the seam allowances toward the darker fabric.

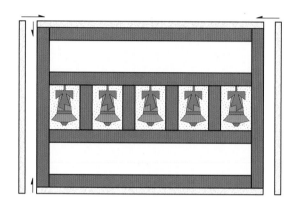

9. Measure the quilt top through the center to determine its width and length. Cut the 7½"-wide middle-border strips to the exact width measurement and stitch to the quilt top and bottom. Press the seam allowances toward the border. Cut two 5½"-wide middle-border strips to the exact length measurement. Stitch a Bell corner block to the ends of each strip, making sure the bells have their longest ribbon streamers to the outside. Stitch the strips to the quilt sides. Press.

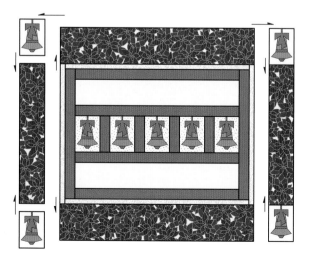

10. Repeat step 8 to add the 3½"-wide outer borders.

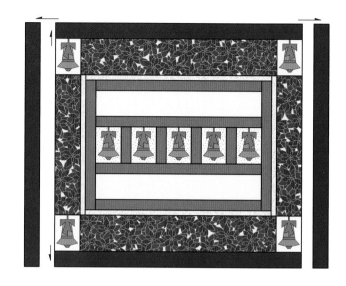

FINISHING YOUR QUILT

Refer to "Finishing" on pages 14–20.

1. Using the patterns on pages 92–93, appliqué the letters for your greeting by hand or machine in the spaces provided. The pictured quilt has 2"-tall letters. Refer to "Appliqué" on page 15 if needed.
2. Cut and piece the backing fabric vertically. Layer the quilt top with batting and backing; baste.
3. Quilt as desired.
4. Square up the quilt top.
5. Add a rod pocket and bind the quilt.
6. Embellish with buttons as desired.
7. Stitch a "Christmas card" label to the quilt back.

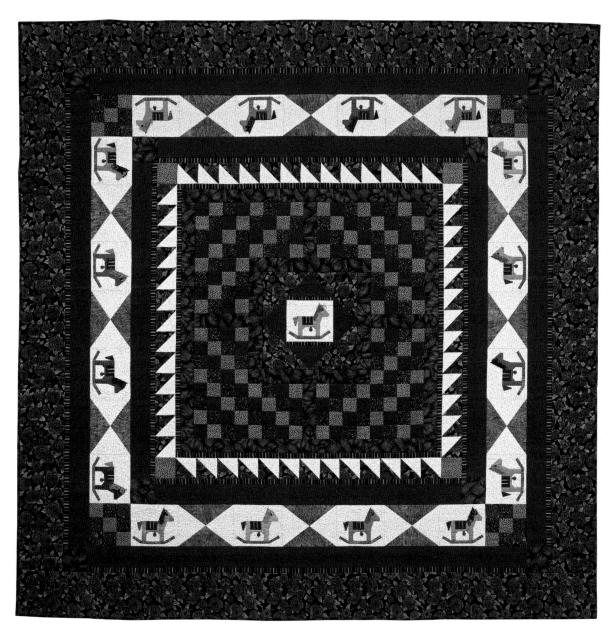

Quilt size: 85½" x 85½"

What little boy or girl wouldn't love this quilt with its brightly colored band of rocking horses? Gather up all your rose-print fabrics, and create this extra-special medallion-style quilt with multiple pieced borders. Encircle the center steed with a whole corral of 16 Rocking Horse blocks. Make them all alike, or go for variety with Appaloosas, Morgans, quarter horses, palominos, pintos, or Arabians; or create your own wild and crazy herd of stripes, polka dots, and candy-bright colored favorites.

Watch the race unfold: On your mark . . . get set . . . they're off!

"For this jubilant Yuletide, may your heart be memory filled."

MATERIALS: 42"-wide fabric

2¾ yards for outer border

2½ yards for block background, half-square triangles, and Hourglass blocks (template G)

1½ yards for inner border

1⅜ yards for sashing and binding

¾ yard for accent borders

⅝ yard for alternate fabric in Hourglass blocks (template H)

⅝ yard of a light-medium value fabric for checkerboard

½ yard of a darker value fabric for checkerboard

⅜ yard of a medium value fabric for checkerboard

4" x 11" for each horse

5" x 5" for each blanket

Scraps for rockers, saddles, and tails

7¾ yards for backing and rod pocket

92" x 92" piece of batting

Embroidery floss for mane

17 buttons, ¼" diameter, for eyes

17 buttons, ⅜" diameter, for stirrups

Template plastic

CUTTING

From the accent-border fabric, cut:
  2 strips, 1" x 7½"
  2 strips, 1¼" x 38½"
  2 strips, 1¼" x 40"
  12 strips, 1¼" x 42"; crosscut 4 into:
    8 strips, 1¼" x 21"

From the inner-border fabric, cut:
  2 squares, 5⅞" x 5⅞"; cut in half diagonally once to make 4 triangles
  12 strips, 3½" x 42"; crosscut 4 into:
    8 strips, 3½" x 21"

From the outer-border fabric, cut:
  4 lengthwise strips, 7½" x 90"
  2 squares, 7⅞" x 7⅞"; cut in half diagonally once to make 4 triangles
  26 squares, 3⅞" x 3⅞"
  8 squares, 2½" x 2½"

From the sashing and binding fabric, cut:
  3 strips, 2½" x 42"; crosscut into:
    2 strips, 2½" x 14½"
    2 strips, 2½" x 18½"
    4 strips, 2½" x 8½"
  2 strips, 2½" x 34½"
  2 strips, 2½" x 38½"
  1 strip, 4¼" x 42"; crosscut into:
    8 squares, 4¼" x 4¼"
  9 strips, 2" x 42", for binding

From the light-medium checkerboard fabric, cut:
  5 strips, 2½" x 42"; crosscut into:
    80 squares, 2½" x 2½"
  4 squares, 3½" x 3½"

From the medium checkerboard fabric, cut:
  4 strips, 2½" x 42"; crosscut into:
    64 squares, 2½" x 2½"

From the darkest checkerboard fabric, cut:
  5 strips, 2½" x 42"; crosscut into:
    76 squares, 2½" x 2½"

From the background, half-square triangles, and Hourglass block fabric, cut:
  3 strips, 3⅞" x 42"; crosscut into:
    26 squares, 3⅞" x 3⅞"
  3 strips, 4¾" x 42"

From the alternate Hourglass block fabric, cut:
  4 strips, 3⅝" x 42"

ASSEMBLY

1. Trace 17 copies of the Rocking Horse foundation pattern on pullout page 1B onto freezer paper.

2. Refer to "Successful Paper Foundation Piecing" on pages 7–14 to construct the blocks, following the sewing order and fabric key on page 33. The blocks should measure 7½" x 6½".

3. Select one Rocking Horse block for the center medallion. Add 1" x 7½" strips of accent fabric to the top and bottom edges. Press the seam allowances toward the accent border.

4. Stitch an inner-border triangle to each side of the center medallion. Press the seam allowances toward the triangles.

5. Stitch an outer-border triangle to each side of the center medallion. Press the seam allowances toward the outer-border triangles.

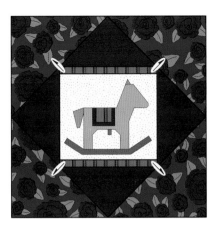

6. Stitch the 2½" x 14½" sashing pieces to the sides of the unit from step 5. Press toward the sashing. Stitch the 2½" x 18½" sashing pieces to the top and bottom. Press.

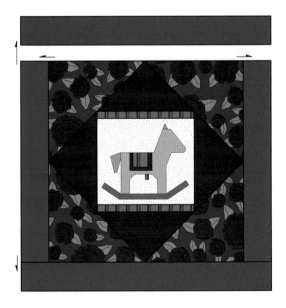

7. Using the 2½" x 2½" squares cut from the three checkerboard fabrics, stitch 12 Sixteen Patch blocks in the two arrangements shown. Make 4 A blocks and 8 B blocks. Press the seams of the

squares in opposite directions from row to row. Press the rows all in one direction.

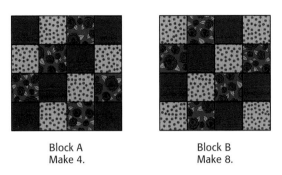

Block A
Make 4.

Block B
Make 8.

8. Arrange the blocks as shown, adding 2½" x 8½" sashing strips to the center of each side. Rotate the blocks to achieve the correct color arrangement and design. Sew and press the seams toward the sashing units.

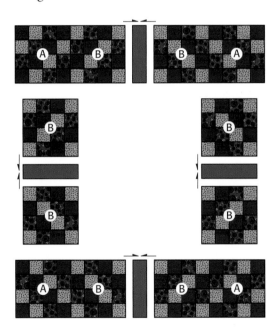

9. Stitch the vertical block–sashing rows to the quilt sides. Press the seams toward the sashing. Stitch the horizontal block–sashing rows to the top and bottom of the quilt. Press.

10. Stitch the 2½" x 34½" sashing strips to the quilt sides. Press the seam allowances toward the sashing. Stitch the 2½" x 38½" sashing strips to the quilt top and bottom. Press.

11. Stitch the 1¼" x 38½" accent-border strips to the quilt sides. Press the seam allowances toward the sashing. Stitch the 1¼" x 40" accent-border strips

to the quilt top and bottom edges. Press toward the sashing.

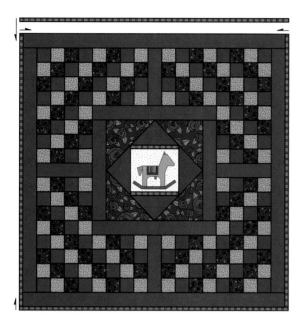

12. To make the 3"-wide half-square-triangle border, use the 3⅞" x 3⅞" squares of the outer-border and background fabrics. Use a ruler and a fabric marking pencil or pen to draw a diagonal line from the upper corner to the lower corner on the wrong side of the background squares.

13. Layer an outer-border square and a background square right sides together with the marked background fabric on top. Sew a diagonal seam ¼" away from the marked line on both sides.

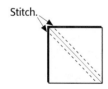

Stitch.

14. Cut along the marked line. Open the fabrics and press the seam allowances toward the darker fabric. Trim off the corner "tails" or "dog ears."

Trim "dog ears."

15. Sew 13 half-square-triangle units together as shown to make one border. Repeat to make four.

Make 4.

16. Stitch two of the half-square-triangle borders to the quilt sides, making sure that the bases of the lighter triangles are toward the center of the quilt and the outer-border triangles are away from the center. Press the seam allowances toward the accent border. Stitch a 3½" x 3½" corner square of the light-medium checkerboard fabric to each end of the remaining half-square-triangle borders, and stitch to the top and bottom edges of the quilt. Press.

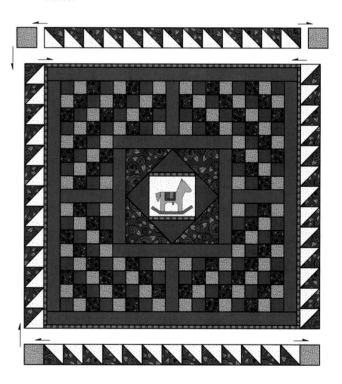

17. To make the strip-pieced borders, stitch a 1¼" x 42" accent-border strip and a 1¼" x 21" accent-border strip together end to end to make one long strip. Make eight. Repeat with the 3½" inner-border strips. Make eight long strips. Stitch a 1¼"-wide accent strip to a 3½"-wide inner-border strip.

Make eight. Press the seam allowances toward the wider strip.

Make 8.

18. Measure the quilt top through the center to determine the length and width. Cut two strip-pieced borders to the measured length and stitch to the quilt sides with the accent fabric to the inside. Press the seam allowances toward the accent border. Cut two remaining strip-pieced borders to the width measurement, and stitch the 4¼" x 4¼" corner squares of sashing fabric to each of the ends. Stitch these pieced strips to the quilt top and bottom. Press the seam allowances toward the accent border. Measure the quilt top through the center and trim it to 52½" x 52½" before adding the next border.

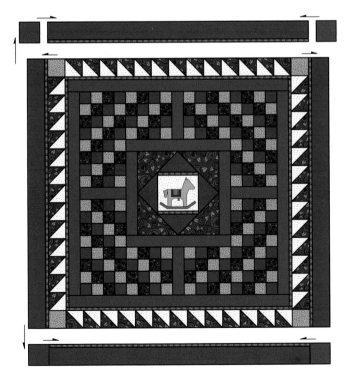

19. **The pieced rocking-horse border:** Make templates out of template plastic from the patterns G and H on pullout page 2B. To make the 8" x 6" Hourglass blocks, lay template G on the 4¾" x 42" strips of the background fabric, and cut out 24

triangles, alternating the triangle direction with each cut. Repeat to cut 24 triangles using template H and the 3⅜" x 42" strips of the alternate Hourglass block fabric.

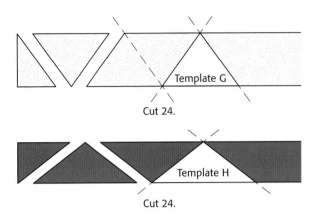

Template G
Cut 24.

Template H
Cut 24.

20. Sew a G and an H triangle together as shown. Press the seam allowances toward the template H triangle. Make 24. Stitch 2 GH units together to make the Hourglass block. Press the seam allowances open. Make 12. Each block should measure 8½" x 6½".

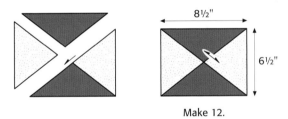

8½"

6½"

Make 12.

21. Alternately stitch together 4 Rocking Horse blocks and 3 Hourglass blocks, as shown. Make sure the horses are all upright and facing the same direction. Press the seam allowances open. Make four. Stitch a pieced border to the quilt sides. Press the seam allowances toward the strip-pieced border.

Make 4.

22. To make the Nine Patch corner blocks, use two outer-border squares (2½" x 2½"), three light-medium checkerboard fabric squares (2½" x 2½"),

and four of the darkest checkerboard fabric squares (2½" x 2½"). Stitch together as shown. Make four.

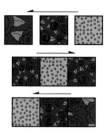 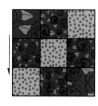

Make 4.

23. Sew a Nine Patch corner block to each end of the remaining Rocking Horse–Hourglass borders, rotating the corner blocks as shown in the quilt diagram. Stitch the borders to the top and bottom of the quilt.

24. Measure the quilt top through the center to determine its length and width. Cut two strip-pieced border units to the exact length measurement and stitch to the quilt sides with the accent-border strip to the outside. Press the seam allowances toward the outer border. Cut the two remaining strip-pieced border units to the width measurement and stitch the 4¼" x 4¼" sashing fabric corner squares to each end. Stitch the pieced strips to the quilt top and bottom with the accent-border strip to the outside. Press.

25. Measure the quilt top through the center to determine the length. Cut two outer-border strips to that exact measurement and stitch to the quilt sides. Press the seams toward the outer borders. Measure the quilt through the center to determine the width. Cut two outer-border strips to that exact measurement and stitch to the quilt top and bottom. Press.

FINISHING YOUR QUILT

Refer to "Finishing" on pages 14–20.

1. Embroider and couch each rocking horse's mane. (See page 15 for details.)
2. Piece the backing fabric vertically. Layer the quilt top with batting and backing; baste.
3. Quilt as desired.
4. Square up the quilt top.
5. Add a rod pocket and bind the quilt.
6. Embellish as desired with beads or buttons for stirrups and eyes.
7. Stitch a "Christmas card" label to the quilt back.

Quilt size: 46" x 84"

Christmas is so many things that delight the senses, and this Yuletide sampler quilt brings them all together, row by row, item by item, memory by memory. Let your eyes feast on each and every block. Let your memories flood back as you create new moments of joy and celebration. Surround yourself with Christmas favorites: angels, snowmen, rocking horses, bells, bows, ornaments, and stars.

"Yuletide thoughts and season's wishes—may you find gladness in each message!"

MATERIALS: 42"-wide fabric

2⅞ yards for block backgrounds (or 1½ yards each of 2 fabrics for more variety)

2½ yards for outer border and binding

1¼ yards for sashing

⅜ yard for inner border

⅛ yard, or scrap, for inner-border corner squares

3 yards for backing

52" x 90" piece of batting

Assorted buttons and beads

Embroidery floss

Appliqué fabrics

MATERIALS FOR BLOCKS

Star (12 blocks)
⅜ yard of fabric (S) for star

Bow (5 blocks)
⅜ yard of fabric (B) for bow

Ornament (6 blocks)
¼ yard of fabric 1 (C1) for ornament

¼ yard of fabric 2 (C2) for ornament

¼ yard of fabric 3 (C3) for ornament

2" x 12" piece of gold fabric (G) for ornament top

Rocking Horse (2 blocks)
5" x 10" piece of fabric (B) for blanket

4" x 22" piece of fabric (H) for horse

3" x 12" piece of fabric (R) for rocker

4" x 8" piece of fabric (S) for saddle

4" x 8" piece of fabric (T) for tail

Angel (3 blocks)
⅜ yard of fabric (D) for dress

6" x 33" piece of fabric 1 (W1) for wing

6" x 33" piece of fabric 2 (W2) for wing

6" x 18" piece of fabric (F) for flesh

5" x 15" piece of fabric (H) for hair

2" x 6" piece of gold fabric (G) for halo

Bells (5 blocks)
¼ yard of fabric (R) for ribbon

¼ yard of fabric (B) for bell

2" x 10" piece of fabric (C) for clapper

Snowman (2 blocks)
8" x 22" piece of fabric (GR) for ground snow

6" x 14" piece of fabric (H) for hat

6" x 12" piece of fabric (M) for mittens

9" x 22" piece of fabric (S) for snowman

7" x 12" piece of fabric (T) for trim

CUTTING

From the sashing fabric, cut:

6 strips, 1½" x 42"; crosscut into:

　15 strips, 1½" x 4½"

　2 strips, 1½" x 15½"

　8 strips, 1½" x 7½"

　2 strips, 1½" x 14½"

12 strips, 2½" x 42"; crosscut 8 into:

　8 strips, 2½" x 29½"

　1 strip, 2½" x 7½"

From the inner-border fabric, cut:

6 strips, 1½" x 42"

From the inner-border–corner-square fabric, cut:

4 squares, 1½" x 1½"

From the outer-border and binding fabric, cut along the lengthwise grain:

2 strips, 6" x 90"

2 strips, 6" x 40"

3 strips, 2" x 90", for binding

ASSEMBLY

1. Using the foundation patterns for the blocks, trace a total of 35 blocks, made up of 12 stars (page 89), 3 angels (page 91 and pullout page 2A), 5 bows (pullout page 1B), 6 ornaments (page 89), 5 bells (pullout page 1B: 2 regular, 3 reversed), 2 snowmen (pages 88–90: 1 regular, 1 reversed), and 2 rocking horses (pullout page 1B: 1 regular, 1 reversed).

2. Refer to "Successful Paper Foundation Piecing" on pages 7–14 to construct the individual blocks, following the sewing order and fabric keys for each. Arrange the blocks as shown.

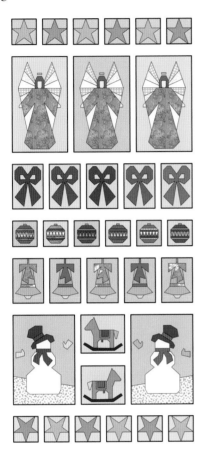

3. Make three horizontal rows of 4" x 4" blocks: two rows of six stars each, and one row of six ornaments. To make each row, alternately sew together six blocks and five 1½" x 4½" sashing strips. Begin and end with a block. Press the seam allowances toward the sashing.

   Note: Make sure the Star blocks are positioned correctly.

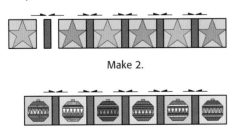

Make 2.

Make 1.

4. Make a horizontal angel row, sewing three Angel blocks and two 1½" x 15½" sashing strips together as shown. Press the seam allowances toward the sashing.

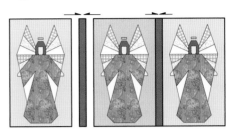

Make 1.

5. Make two horizontal rows of 5" x 7" blocks: one row of five Bow blocks, and one row of five Bell blocks. To make each row, alternately stitch together five blocks and four 1½" x 7½" sashing strips as shown. Press the seam allowances toward the sashing strips.

Make 1.

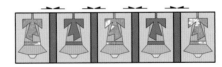

Make 1.

6. Make the snowman and rocking-horse row. Stitch together the two Rocking Horse blocks and the 2½" x 7½" horizontal sashing strip. Press the seam allowances toward the sashing strip. Make sure the rocking horses are standing upright.

   Sew a 1½" x 14½" sashing strip to each side of the Rocking Horse blocks. Press toward the sashing.

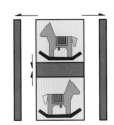

7. Sew a Snowman block to each side of the rocking-horse unit, making sure the snowmen's stick arms are raised toward the center. Press the seams toward the sashing.

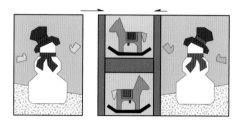

8. Assemble the 2½" x 29½" sashing strips and block rows as shown below. Stitch the rows together. Press the seam allowances toward the sashing.

9. Stitch two sashing strips, 2½" x 42", together end to end to make one long strip. Repeat to make two long strips. Measure the quilt top through the center to determine the length. Cut the two pieced strips to this length. Stitch the strips to the quilt sides. Press toward the sashing.

10. Measure the quilt top through the center to determine the width and length. Cut two inner-border strips to the width measured and stitch to the quilt top and bottom. Press toward the inner border. Stitch two inner-border strips together end to end to make one long strip. Make two. Cut these strips to the quilt length measured before the inner borders were added. Stitch the inner-border corner squares to the ends of the strips. Stitch the pieced strips to the quilt sides. Press.

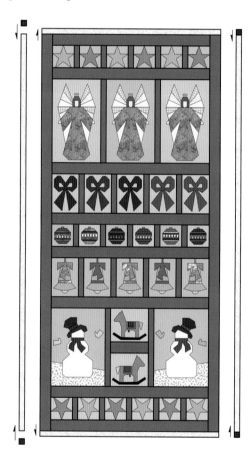

11. Measure the quilt top through the center to determine its width. Cut the 6" x 40" outer-border strips to the exact measurement and stitch to the quilt top and bottom edges. Press the seam allowances toward the outer border. Measure the quilt top through the center to determine its length. Cut the 6" x 90" outer-border strips to the exact measurement and stitch the strips to the quilt sides. Press.

FINISHING YOUR QUILT

Refer to "Finishing" on pages 14–20.

1. Embroider and appliqué any needed details.
2. Piece the backing with a horizontal seam. Layer the quilt top with batting and backing; baste.
3. Quilt as desired.
4. Square up the quilt top.
5. Add a rod pocket and bind the quilt.
6. Add desired bead or button embellishments.
7. Stitch a "Christmas card" label to the quilt back.

Decorator's Alert

This wonderful quilt deserves a spot all its own to showcase your handiwork. Display it prominently in an entryway or in the room where most of your holiday entertaining will be done. It offers plenty of opportunity for creative decorating with your favorite Christmas items.

Quilt size: 34" x 63"

We are all familiar with Santa Claus in his traditional fur-trimmed red suit, but just imagine how he might dress after his long night's journey of rooftop gift delivery. Well, here he is in his old-fashioned red union suit (with its button-up seat), and brown, floppy "mules" on his feet. He's all decked out and ready to hit the sack. It was a great trip, but now he's eager to catch up on his sleep. "Night! Night! Sleep tight!" Shhhh!!!

"Merry Christmas to all . . . and to all a good night!"

MATERIALS: 42"-wide fabric

2 yards for outer border, sashing corner squares, ribbons, and binding

1⅛ yards for block background

1⅛ yards for middle border, long johns, and ornament color 1

⅜ yard for sashing

⅜ yard for inner border

¼ yard for bells

Assorted scraps for slippers, shoe soles, cuffs, flesh, beard, mustache, ornament color 2, ornament color 3, gold, and bell clappers

Scrap for inner-border corner squares

2 yards for backing and rod pocket

40" x 69" piece of batting

Embroidery floss for nose, eyes, and outlining

Bell or button for stocking cap

4 buttons for bell clappers

CUTTING

From the sashing fabric, cut:

    2 strips, 2½" x 42"; crosscut into:

        2 strips, 2½" x 7½"

        4 strips, 2½" x 12½"

    2 strips, 2½" x 41½"*

From the outer-border fabric, cut on the lengthwise grain:

    3 strips, 4½" x 72"; crosscut† 1 into:

        2 strips, 4½" x 26½"

        4 squares, 2½" x 2½"

    3 strips, 2" x 72", for binding

From the inner-border fabric, cut:

    5 strips, 1½" x 42"; crosscut 1 into:

        2 strips, 1½" x 16½"

From the inner-border–corner-square fabric, cut:

    4 squares, 1½" x 1½"

From the middle-border fabric, cut:

    5 strips, 4½" x 42"; crosscut† 1 into:

        2 strips, 4½" x 18½"

If your fabric is not wide enough to cut a 41½" strip, you will need to piece these long sashing strips.

† You may want to wait to cut these strips until you measure and assemble the quilt top.

ASSEMBLY

1. Using the Santa Claus foundation pattern on pull-out page 2B, trace one pattern onto freezer paper.

2. Using the Yuletide Bell foundation pattern on pullout page 1B, trace four patterns onto freezer paper, reversing two.

3. Using the Yuletide Ornament foundation pattern on page 89, trace four patterns onto freezer paper.

4. Refer to "Successful Paper Foundation Piecing" on pages 7–14 to construct the blocks, following the sewing order and fabric keys for each individual block. Trim the Santa block to 12½" x 23½", being sure to center the character. Be sure that the Bell blocks measure 5½" x 7½".

5. To make the two bell rows, stitch together two bells and one 2½" x 7½" sashing strip, making sure the long tails of the ribbons are to the outside. Press the seam allowances toward the sashing.

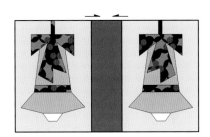

Make 2.

6. Stitch a 2½" x 12½" sashing strip to the top and bottom of the Santa block. Add a bell row above and below. Press the seam allowances toward the sashing.

7. Sew the remaining 2½" x 12½" sashing strips to the top and bottom of the quilt. Press the seam allowances toward the sashing. Stitch a 2½" x 2½" sashing corner square to each short end of the 2½" x 41½" side sashing strips. Stitch the pieced strips to the quilt sides. Press.

8. Measure the quilt through the center to determine the length. Sew the 1½" x 16½" inner-border strips to the top and bottom of the quilt. Press the

seam allowances toward the inner border. Stitch two remaining inner-border strips together end to end to make one long strip. Make two, and cut each strip to the length measured for the quilt sides. Stitch an inner-border corner square to each end of the side strips. Stitch the pieced strips to the quilt sides. Press.

9. Measure the quilt through the center to determine the length and width. Sew the 4½" x 18½" middle-border strips to the top and bottom. Press the seam allowances toward the middle border. Stitch two of the remaining middle-border strips together end to end to make one long strip. Make two. Cut each strip to the length measured for the quilt sides. Stitch a Yuletide Ornament block to the end of these side strips, making sure the ornaments are upright. Stitch the pieced strips to the quilt sides. Press.

10. Stitch the 4½" x 26½" outer-border strips to the quilt top and bottom. Press the seam allowances

toward the outer border. Measure the quilt top through the center to determine the length. Cut the remaining two outer-border strips to the exact measurement and stitch to the sides. Press.

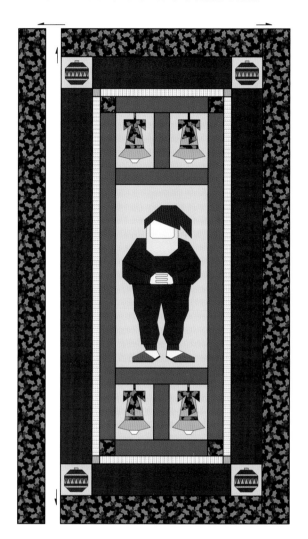

FINISHING YOUR QUILT

Refer to "Finishing" on pages 14–20.

1. Appliqué Santa's mustache and embroider any desired block details.
2. Layer the quilt top with batting and backing; baste.
3. Quilt as desired.
4. Square up the quilt top.
5. Add a rod pocket and bind the quilt.
6. Embellish Santa and the bells with bell and buttons as desired.
7. Stitch a "Christmas card" label to the quilt back.

Season's Greetings
Gingerbread House Banner

Quilt size: 26" x 49½"

Sweets! Treats! Gumdrops! Peppermint candy canes! Gingerbread cookies! All these add up to a taste-tempting recipe for Yuletide cheer. Create a Christmas heirloom and set the mood for the holidays with this delightful gingerbread-house banner. Start with the Winter Cottage foundation pattern, and then begin to celebrate. Choose bright, festive fabrics. Stitch up rows of gingerbread boys and girls and decorated Christmas trees. Embellish with appliquéd holly leaves and button berries, beaded frostings and button candies. And pass along a favorite Yuletide greeting or two.

"Season's Greetings!"

MATERIALS: 42"-wide fabric

1⅜ yards for block and message background

1¼ yards for outer border and binding

½ yard for sashing

⅜ yard for gingerbread girls and boys

⅜ yard for pine trees, or scraps if tree variety is desired

⅛ yard each, or scraps, of 5 assorted fabrics for pieced border

Assorted scraps for house, sidewalk, windows, door and chimney, trim, roof, tree trunks, snow 1, snow 2, and holly leaves

1⅝ yards for backing and rod pocket

32" x 56" piece of batting

Fabric for lettering

Beads, buttons, charms, etc., for gingerbread house, kids, trees, and holly berries

CUTTING*

From *each* of the 5 pieced-border fabrics, cut:
1 strip, 1½" x 42"

From the background fabric, cut:
2 strips, 3½" x 12½"
1 strip, 6½" x 20½"
1 strip, 4½" x 20½"

From the sashing fabric, cut:
5 strips, 1½" x 20½"
2 strips, 1½" x 15"
2 strips, 1½" x 42"

From the outer-border and binding fabric, cut on the lengthwise grain:
1 strip, 3½" x 45"
2 strips, 2½" x 45"
1 strip, 2½" x 45"; crosscut into:
    2 strips, 2½" x 22½"
4 strips, 2" x 45", for binding

You may want to wait until after the blocks are assembled before cutting the other fabrics for the quilt.

ASSEMBLY

1. Using the foundation patterns for the blocks, trace a total of 10 patterns onto freezer paper: 3 gingerbread girls, 2 gingerbread boys, 4 pine trees (all on pullout page 1B), and 1 winter cottage (pullout page 2A).

2. Refer to "Successful Paper Foundation Piecing" on pages 7–14 to construct the individual blocks, following the sewing order and fabric keys for each. The Gingerbread Girl and Boy blocks should each measure 4½" x 5½"; the Pine Tree blocks should measure 5½" x 7½"; and the Winter Cottage block should measure 12½" x 12½". If they do not, trim them to the correct size, or adjust the lengths of the sashing and border strips accordingly.

3. Stitch the five Gingerbread Girl and Boy blocks together in a row, alternating girls and boys, as shown. Press the seam allowances open.

4. Stitch the four Pine Tree blocks together in a row. Press the seam allowances open.

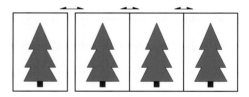

5. To make the pieced borders, stitch the 1½" x 42" assorted fabric strips together along the lengthwise edges to make a strip set. Press all the seam allowances in the same direction.

6. Using your rotary cutter and ruler, crosscut the pieced unit into 1½"-wide segments. Stitch the

segments together end to end. Make four strips of 20 squares each, and two strips of 12 squares each. Use a seam ripper to remove squares as needed.

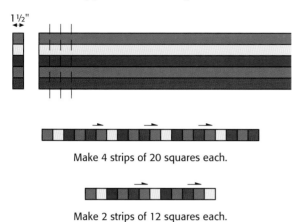

1½"

Make 4 strips of 20 squares each.

Make 2 strips of 12 squares each.

7. Stitch a 20-square pieced border to the top and bottom edges of the gingerbread row and to the top and bottom of the pine-tree row. Press the seam allowances toward the pieced borders.

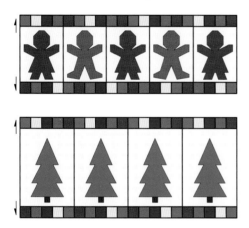

8. To make the gingerbread-house row, stitch a 12-square pieced border strip to each side of the Winter Cottage block. Stitch a 3½" x 12½" message panel to each side of the pieced border. Press the seams toward the pieced borders.

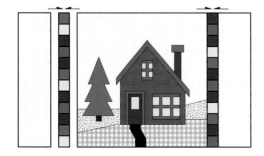

9. To make the pointed message panel at the bottom of the quilt, fold the 6½" x 20½" panel in half so that it is 6½" x 10¼". With a ruler, carefully mark a point on the cut sides 2½" down from the top edge. Using a rotary cutter and ruler, cut a diagonal line from that point down to the center fold at the bottom edge. Open the panel.

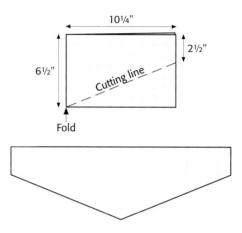

10¼"

2½"

6½"

Cutting line

Fold

10. Stitch a 1½" x 20½" sashing strip between each of the assembled rows and the 4½" x 20½" message panel, as shown. Press the seam allowances toward the sashing strips.

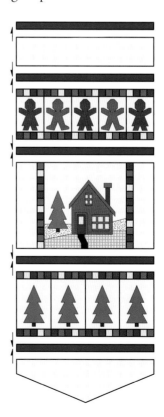

11. Add the 1½" x 15" sashing strips to the angled bottom edges of the quilt, leaving excess length at the center point. Stop stitching ¼" from the center point. Backstitch, being careful not to sew into the seam allowance of the center point. Miter the center point (see below) and trim the ends even with the sides. Press the seam allowances toward the sashing.

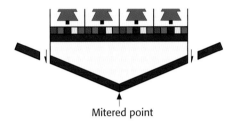

Mitered point

Mitering the Center Point

To miter the center-point border strips, carefully fold the quilt top in half at the center with border strips aligned right sides together.

★ Carefully pick out any stitches in the seam allowance at the center point. Pin the strips together.

★ With a ruler and fabric marker, carefully draw in the seam line, which is the extension of the fold line. Begin stitching at the inner center point, securing the seam with a backstitch. Sew to the outside edge of the border strips.

★ After sewing, unfold the quilt top and check the seam to see that it is straight. Trim the excess border strips, leaving a ¼" seam allowance. Press the seam open.

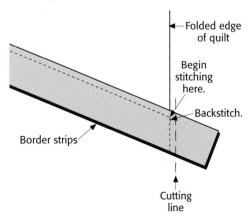

← Folded edge of quilt

Begin stitching here.

Backstitch.

Border strips

Cutting line

12. Stitch a 1½" x 42" sashing strip to each side of the quilt. Trim the end at the same angle as the bottom diagonal sashing. Press the seam allowances toward the sashing.

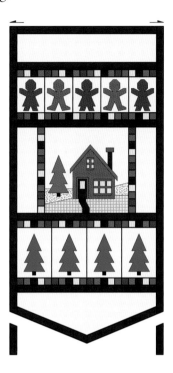

13. Stitch the 2½" x 22½" outer-border strips to the diagonal bottom edges, mitering the center point as you did for the sashing. Trim the excess fabric at the sides even with the side sashing. Press the seam allowances toward the outer border.

14. Measure the quilt length at the sides. Cut two 2½" x 45" outer-border strips to that measurement and stitch to the quilt sides. Press the seam allowances toward the borders. Trim the end at the same angle as the bottom diagonal border.

15. Measure the quilt top through the center to determine the width. Cut the 3½"-wide outer-border strip to the exact measurement and stitch to the top of the banner. Press the seam allowance toward the outer border.

FINISHING YOUR QUILT

Refer to "Finishing" on pages 14–20.

1. Appliqué by hand or machine any messages or designs desired in the message panels, using the alphabet patterns on pages 92–93 if you wish. Using the holly-leaf pattern below, scatter holly leaves along the side message panels and appliqué them to the background.
2. Layer the quilt top with batting and backing; baste.
3. Quilt as desired.
4. Square up the quilt top.
5. Add a rod pocket and bind the quilt.
6. Embellish as desired with beads, buttons, and charms. Add red buttons among the holly leaves to serve as holly berries.
7. Stitch a "Christmas card" label to the quilt back.

Holly Leaf
Cut 19.

Appliqué Pattern

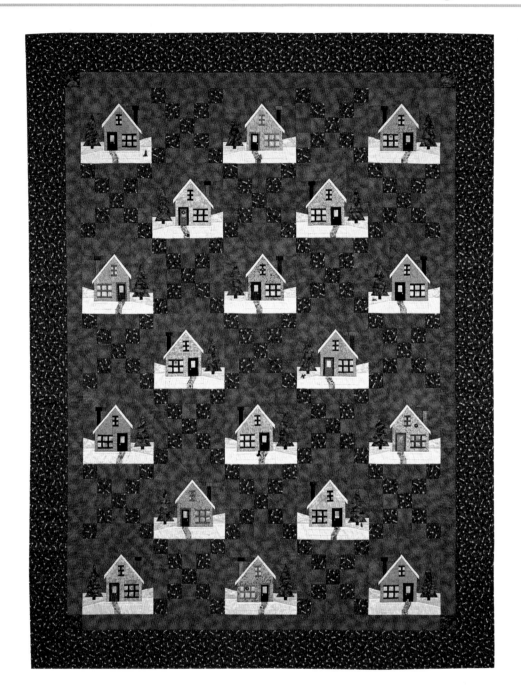

Quilt size: 77" x 101"

Feast your eyes on the candles all aglow in this wonderland of cottages. Each one is alight with the yuletide spirit of warmth and hospitality. The Single Irish Chain alternate blocks serve as the illuminated pathway that lights your way through the neighborhood while each home says "welcome" and "enjoy" with well-lit doors and windows. Come in. Sit. Stay awhile! Take a moment to celebrate the Yuletide season with the neighborhood!

"Though the winds may blow and the snow may fall,
may you always find warmth inside these cozy winter cottages."

MATERIALS: 42"-wide fabric

4⅝ yards for block background and Single Irish Chain blocks

3 yards for outer border and binding

2 yards for snow 1 and roofs

1½ yards for snow 2

1½ yards for windows

1½ yards for trim (or scraps for color variety)

1½ yards for cottages (or scraps for color variety)

1⅛ yards for Single Irish Chain blocks

⅞ yard for pine trees

⅞ yard for inner border

⅝ yard for sidewalks

⅝ yard for doors and chimneys (or scraps for color variety)

4" x 15" piece or scrap for inner-border corner squares

Scrap for tree trunks

6½ yards for backing and rod pocket

84" x 108" piece of batting

Assorted buttons and beads for door handles and cottage decoration

CUTTING

From the Irish Chain fabric, cut:

12 strips, 2⅞" x 42"; crosscut into:

153 squares, 2⅞" x 2⅞"

From the background fabric, cut:

21 strips, 2⅞" x 42"; crosscut into:

272 squares, 2⅞" x 2⅞"

From the inner-border fabric, cut:

8 strips, 3" x 42"

From the inner-border–corner-square fabric, cut:

4 squares, 3" x 3"

From the outer-border and binding fabric, cut on the lengthwise grain:

4 strips, 6½" x 108"

4 strips, 2" x 108", for binding

ASSEMBLY

1. Using the foundation pattern for the Winter Cottage block on pullout page 2A, trace 18 patterns (9 regular and 9 reversed) onto freezer paper.

2. Refer to "Successful Paper Foundation Piecing" on pages 7–14 to construct the blocks, following the sewing order and fabric key on page 36. The blocks should measure 12½" x 12½".

3. To construct the Single Irish Chain blocks, arrange the 2⅞" squares as shown below.

4. Stitch the squares together in rows. Press seam allowances in opposite directions from row to row.

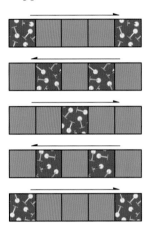

Stitcher's Alert

Be sure that you are stitching with an accurate ¼" seam allowance. For these blocks made up of 25 squares, any slight variance in your seams will affect the overall size of the completed blocks. You may want to measure your completed Irish Chain blocks to get an average size. Trim the Winter Cottage blocks to that size.

5. Stitch the rows together, pressing the seam allowances all in one direction. Make 17. The blocks should measure 12½" x 12½".

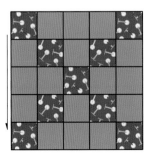

Make 17.

6. Arrange the Winter Cottage blocks as desired, noting the placement of the pine trees and the colors of the cottages.

7. To make block rows 1, 3, 5, and 7, alternately stitch together three Winter Cottage blocks, and two Irish Chain blocks as shown. Press the seam allowances toward the cottages.

Make 4.

8. To make block rows 2, 4, and 6, alternately stitch together three Irish Chain blocks and two Winter Cottage blocks, as shown. Press the seam allowances toward the cottages.

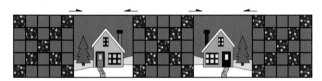

Make 3.

9. Arrange the block rows in numerical order and stitch together. Press the seam allowances all in one direction.

10. Stitch two inner-border strips together end to end to make one long strip. Make four. Measure the quilt through the center to determine the length and width. Cut two pieced strips to the length measured. Stitch the strips to the quilt sides. Press the seam allowances toward the border. Cut the two remaining pieced border strips to the width measured. Stitch the inner-border corner squares to each end of the strip. Sew the strips to the top and bottom of the quilt. Press.

11. Measure the quilt top through the center to determine the length. Cut two 6½" x 108" outer-border strips to the exact measurement and stitch to the quilt sides. Press the seams toward the outer border. Measure the quilt top through the center to determine the width. Cut the remaining outer-border strips to the exact measurement and stitch the strips to the top and bottom of the quilt. Press.

FINISHING YOUR QUILT

Refer to "Finishing" on pages 14–20.

1. Piece the backing fabric horizontally. Layer the quilt top with batting and backing; baste.

2. Quilt as desired.

3. Square up the quilt top.

4. Add a rod pocket and bind the quilt.

5. Embellish with buttons and beads as desired.

6. Stitch a "Christmas card" label to the quilt back.

Simple Christmas Joys Gallery

Stitch up some quick holiday cheer by adding one or more borders to any of the blocks. For a slightly more complex design, combine blocks or use some of the 4" designs in the border.

Dudley, the Christmas Nutcracker

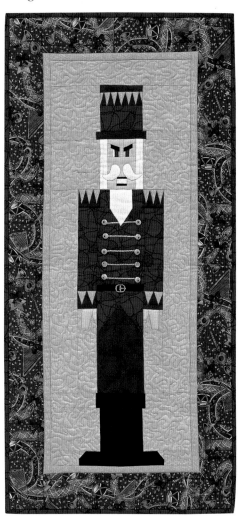

Quilt size: 16" x 33"

His gaze looks so fierce! His teeth so sharp! His demeanor so terribly ferocious! Dudley has a job to do, and he does it very well. He opens nuts with one mighty crunch and one powerful crack! Can't you just taste the sweet, nutty flavors hidden inside?

"Let this nutcracker help you enjoy a tasty Yuletide season!"

Radiant Angel

Quilt size: 18" x 24"

Let this well-dressed angel announce the Christmas season for you, and all your celebrations! Dress her all in gold and white as a truly elegant holiday delight, or choose a gloriously colorful fabric to make the season bright. Make one jubilant block for a small wall quilt, or make "multitudes of angels" all in a row.

"Angels we have heard on high!"

Lawrence Russell, Yuletide Snowman

Quilt size: 21" x 25"

Do you remember the joy of building your very own snowman? How hard it was to roll up those big, bigger, biggest balls of snow? Remember searching through the old winter clothes to find that perfect top hat, scarf, and mittens for your snow character? Or raiding Mom's refrigerator for the carrot nose? And then there was the search for the perfect tree branches to serve as scraggly arms. Do you remember?

Bring back those memories when you create this Yuletide snowman, but in the comfort of your warm, cozy sewing room. Welcome this fellow in, and what a treat—he won't melt with the coming of spring!

"Dress warmly! Hug often! Be creative! Celebrate!"

Mrs. Santa Claus

Quilt size: 24½" x 31½"

Mrs. Claus . . . Mrs. Claus. We hear so much about Santa Claus, but what about Mrs. Claus? We know she's back at the North Pole baking up a storm, keeping all the elves full of cookies and candies, and watching out for Santa's health and well-being. We know she must be a kindly, gentle person with a cheerful smile on her face, creating a warm, cozy, and welcoming home for Santa.

Why, here she is! All dressed up in her Yuletide dress and apron, with a cozy cap on her head. And she's been baking a tasty Christmas pie, just for us!

"Mmm . . . mmm . . . yumm . . . May all the aromas of your Yuletide celebrations be warm and delicious."

Winter Cottage

Quilt size: 21" x 21"

*Nothing seems quite so cheerful on a
cold, snowy winter night as seeing a cozy
cottage lit up with windows all aglow.
This small wall quilt seems to say,
"Welcome. Glad you are here!" Make
this wintry Christmas scene with a
holiday wreath on the door or window
and a starry night sky above.
This small winter cottage lends
warmth and charm to your
holiday decorating.*

*"The road that leads to Christmas
is lined with memories. Welcome
home for the holidays!"*

Yuletide Bell

Quilt size: 13" x 15"

*Stitch up this simple bell block, wrap multiple
borders of color around it, and share it
with that special friend.*

*"Ring in the Christmas season
with great musical joy!"*

Rocking Horse Delight

Quilt size: 15" x 14"

*This little pony is the perfect size for a small Yuletide
wall quilt, or perhaps a holiday pillow.*

*"May all the rides of your life be as joyous as the
ones you experienced on your childhood rocking horse!"*

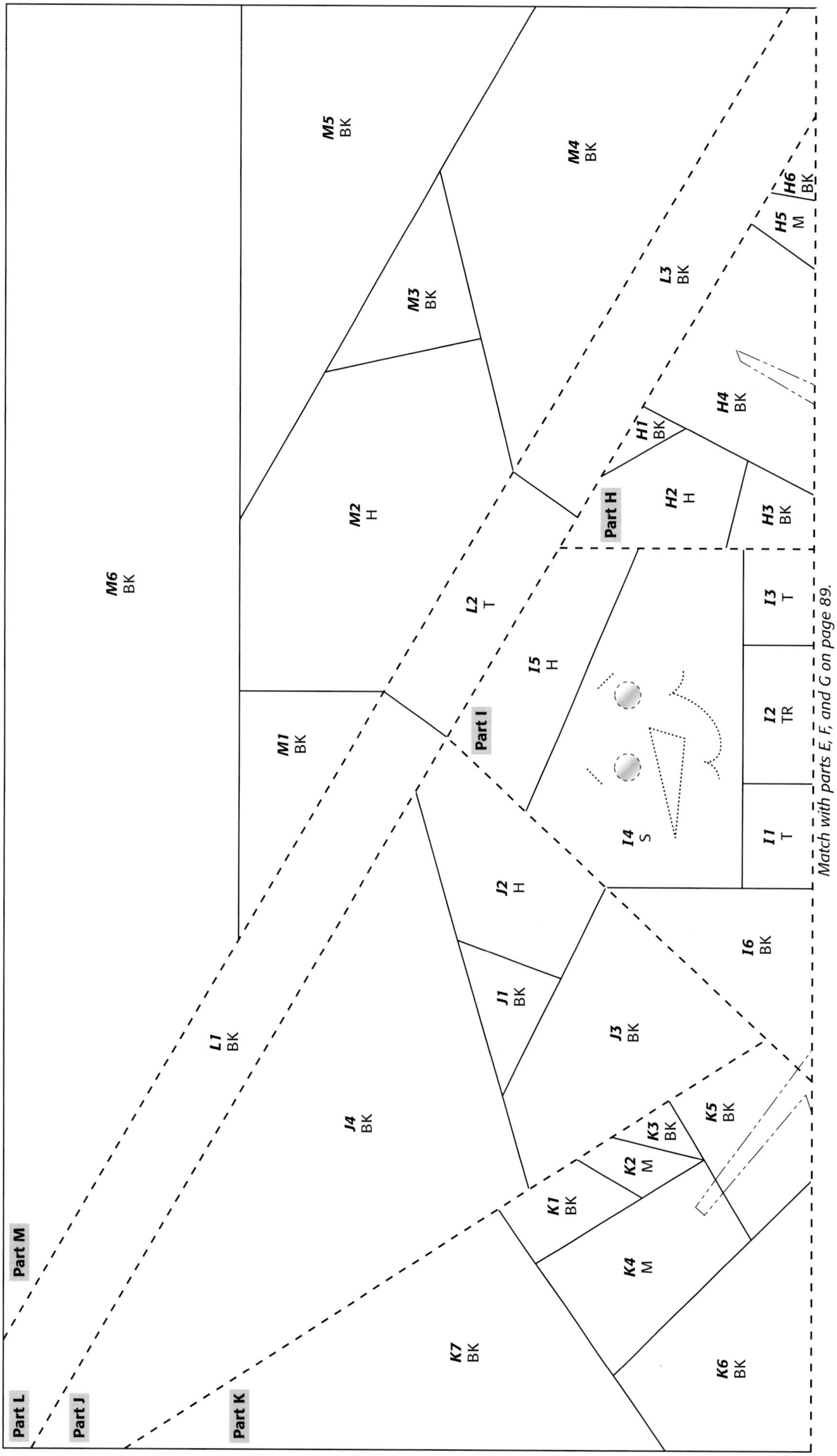

M5
BK

M4
BK

H5
M

H6
BK

M3
BK

L3
BK

H4
BK

H1
BK

M2
H

Part H

H2
H

H3
BK

M6
BK

L2
T

I5
H

I3
T

I2
TR

Part I

I1
T

M1
BK

I4
S

J2
H

I6
BK

J1
BK

J3
BK

L1
BK

K5
BK

J4
BK

K3
BK

K2
M

K1
BK

K4
M

Part M

K7
BK

K6
BK

Part L

Part J

Part K

Match with parts E, F, and G on page 89.

Lawrence Russell,
Yuletide Snowman
Parts H, I, J, K, L, and M

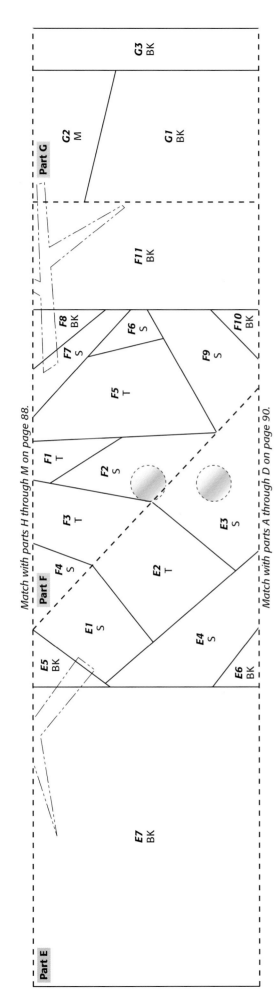

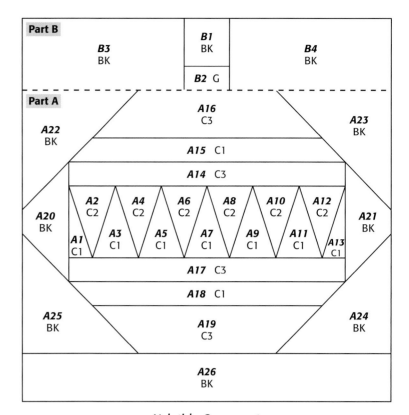

Yuletide Ornament

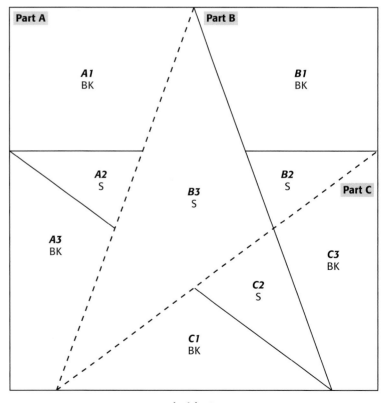

Yuletide Star

Lawrence Russell,
Yuletide Snowman
Parts E, F, and G

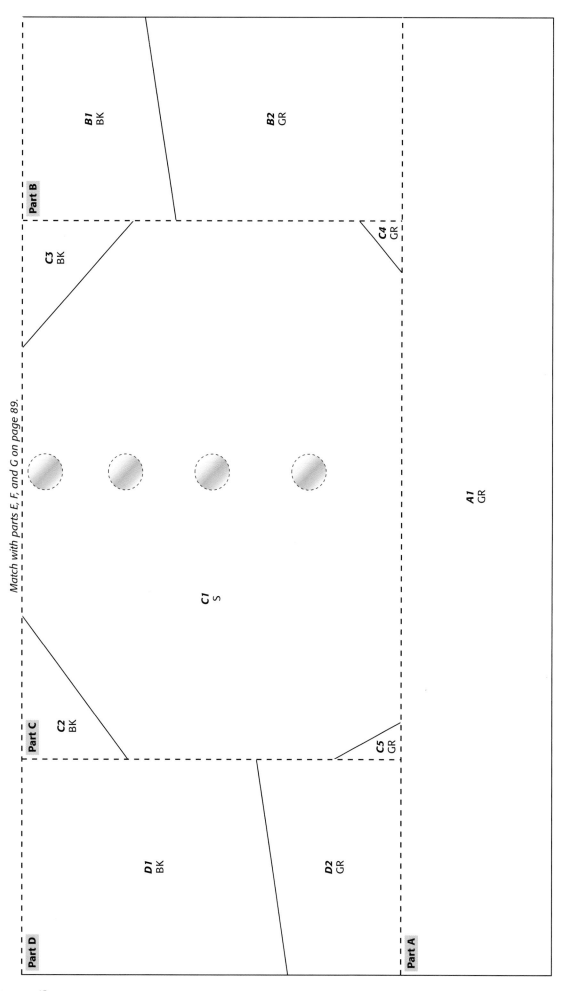

Part B

B1 BK

B2 GR

C3 BK

C4 GR

Match with parts E, F, and G on page 89.

A1 GR

C1 S

Part C

C2 BK

C5 GR

D1 BK

D2 GR

Part D

Part A

Lawrence Russell,
Yuletide Snowman
Parts A, B, C, and D

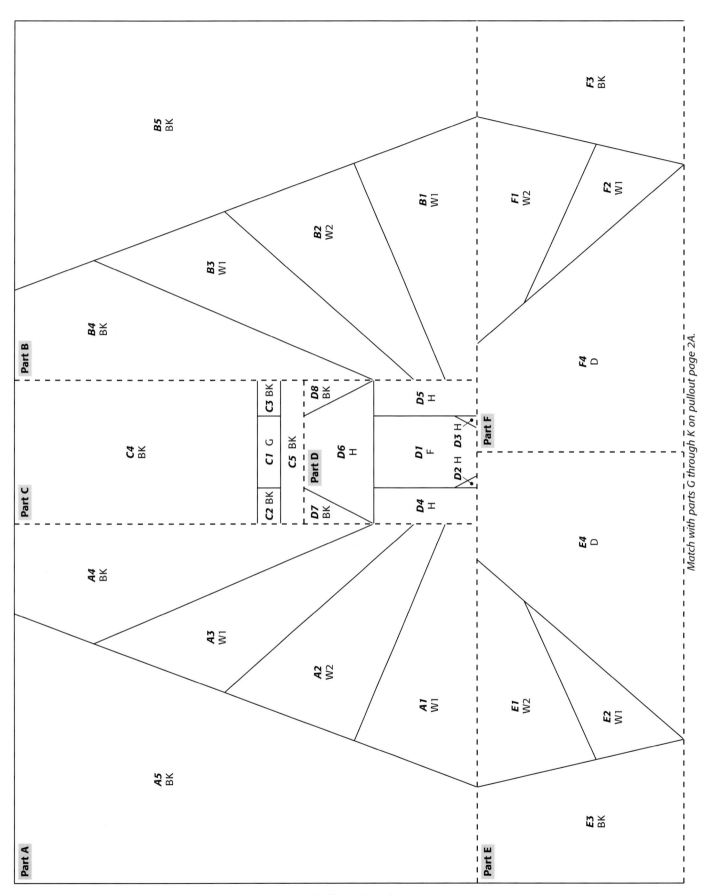

Radiant Angel
Parts A, B, C, D, E, and F

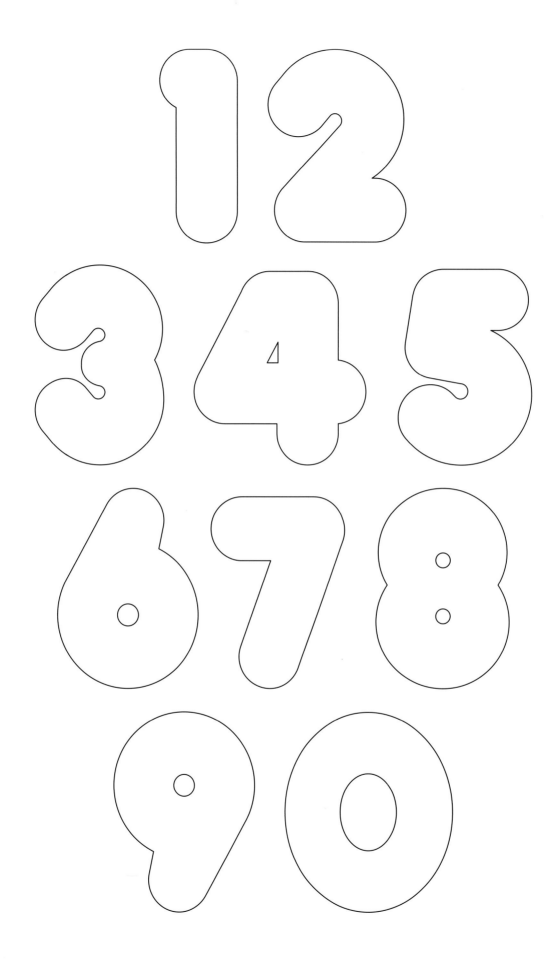

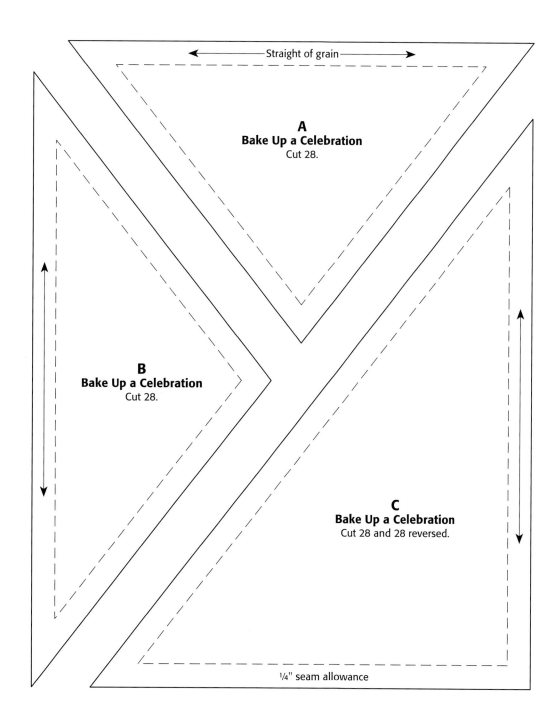

Straight of grain

A
Bake Up a Celebration
Cut 28.

B
Bake Up a Celebration
Cut 28.

C
Bake Up a Celebration
Cut 28 and 28 reversed.

¼" seam allowance

About the Author

Jaynette Huff has been quilting since 1974; she takes great pleasure in all aspects of the process. For the last several years she has focused her interests on translating landscapes and architecture into pieced quilts. Most recently, miniature quilts have captured her imagination.

Jaynette's first career was teaching high school English and speech. She then studied business management and taught at the college level for twelve years before opening her own quilt shop in 1992. She closed the shop in 2001 in order to write quilt books, teach quilting, and work on her own projects full-time.

Jaynette has written two other books on paper foundation piecing: *Needles and Notions* (2000) and *For the Birds* (2001), both published by Martingale & Company. Jaynette enjoys traveling to teach and lecture about quilts, as well as designing and creating her own works for competition. She also creates quilted paraments and banners for her church.

She lives with her husband, Larry, in Conway, Arkansas, where he teaches mathematics at the University of Central Arkansas. They enjoy spending their free time at their farm in South Dakota.